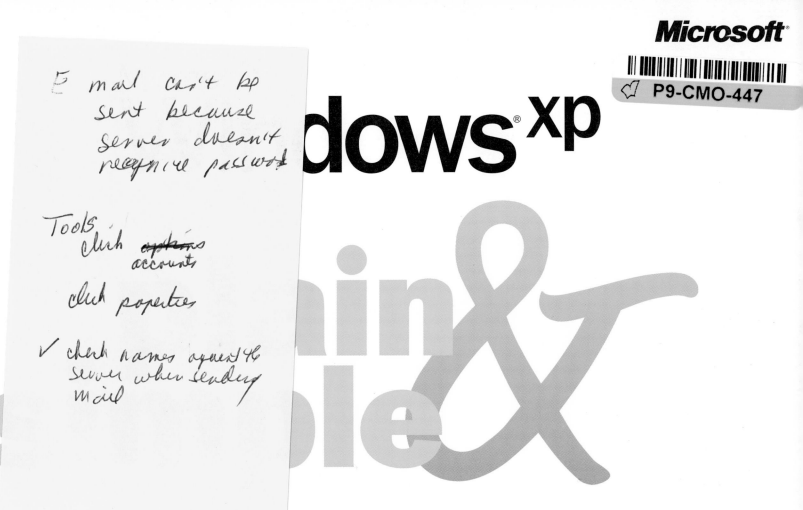

Microsoft®

P9-CMO-447

dows® xp

in &
ble

Your fast-answers, no-jargon
guide to Windows XP!

Jerry Joyce &
Marianne Moon

Handwritten note:

5 mail can't be
sent because
server doesn't
recognize password

Tools
click options
accounts

click properties

✓ check names against the
server when sending
mail

PUBLISHED BY
Microsoft Press
A Division of Microsoft Corporation
One Microsoft Way
Redmond, Washington 98052-6399

Library of Congress Cataloging-in-Publication Data
Joyce, Jerry, 1950-
    Microsoft Windows XP Plain & Simple / Jerry Joyce, Marianne Moon.
        p. cm.
    Includes index.
    ISBN 0-7356-1525-X
    1. Microsoft Windows XP.   2. Operating systems (Computers)   I. Title: Microsoft
Windows XP Plain and Simple.   II. Moon, Marianne.   III. Title.

QA76.76.O63 J695   2001
005.4'4769--dc21   2001044698

Printed and bound in the United States of America.

2 3 4 5 6 7 8 9   QWT   6 5 4 3 2 1

Distributed in Canada by Penguin Books Canada Limited.

A CIP catalogue record for this book is available from the British Library.

Microsoft Press books are available through booksellers and distributors worldwide. For further information about international editions, contact your local Microsoft Corporation office or contact Microsoft Press International directly at fax (425) 936-7329. Visit our Web site at www.microsoft.com/mspress. Send comments to *mspinput@microsoft.com*.

Acquisitions Editor: Kong Cheung
Project Editor: Kristen Weatherby
Technical Editor: Jerry Joyce
Manuscript Editor: Marianne Moon

Body Part No. X08-29520

Contents

4 · Exploring the Internet · 43

5 · Communicating · 53

6 Working with Pictures and Movies 75

7 Working with Music, Voice, and Sounds 97

8 Printing and Faxing 111

9 Managing Files and Folders 125

10 Networking · 145

11 Setting Up · 163

14 Managing Windows XP 207

i Index 229

Acknowledgments

This book is the result of the combined efforts of a team of people whose work we trust and admire and whose friendship we value highly. Kristin Ziesemer, our talented typographer, did the work of two people and did it superbly. She not only refined and produced the interior graphics but also laid out the complex design, wrestling heroically with problems ranging from limited space to logical arrangement of numbered steps. We think she does beautiful work. Our dear friend Alice Copp Smith has helped us improve every book we've written. Alice does so much more than proofread and copyedit: her gentle and witty chiding on countless yellow sticky notes makes us groan but always teaches us to write better. And we are fortunate indeed to be able to work with indexer extraordinaire Caroline Parks, whose index reveals in microcosm the soul of the book. We thank this dedicated and hard-working trio for their exceptional work and their unwavering good humor in the face of grueling deadlines.

At Microsoft Press we thank Kong Cheung for asking us to write this book, and we thank Kristen Weatherby for her valuable insight and helpful suggestions. Thanks also to Jim Kramer, Gregory Beckelhymer, Kevin Coomes, and Candace Jorgensen, all of whom provided assistance and advice along the way.

On the home front, as always, Roberta Moon-Krause, Rick Krause, and Zuzu Abeni Krause provided love, laughter, and inspiration. We also thank the Krause puppies, Baiser and Pierre, for being gracious enough to allow us to publish their private playlist and to chat with us over the Internet.

We dedicate this book to the memory of Sachin Krause,
who will live in our hearts forever.

1 About This Book

If you want to get the most from your computer and your software with the least amount of time and effort—and who doesn't?—this book is for you. You'll find *Microsoft Windows XP Plain & Simple* to be a straight-forward, easy-to-read reference tool. With the premise that your computer should work for you, not you for it, this book's purpose is to help you get your work done quickly and efficiently so that you can get away from the computer and live your life. Our book is based on the Home Edition of Microsoft Windows XP, but if you're running Windows XP Professional, you can still use the information you'll find here. Of course, our book doesn't deal with some of the Professional version's features—joining a domain and working with offline network files, for example.

No Computerese!

Let's face it—when there's a task you don't know how to do but you need to get it done in a hurry, or when you're stuck in the middle of a task and can't figure out what to do next, there's nothing more frustrating than having to read page after page of technical background material. You want the information you need—nothing more, nothing less—and you want it now! *And* it should be easy to find and understand.

That's what this book is all about. It's written in plain English—no technical jargon and no computerese. No single task in the book takes more than two pages. Just look the task up in the index or the table of contents, turn to the page, and there's the information you need, laid out in an illustrated step-by-step format. You don't get bogged down by the whys and wherefores: just follow the steps and get your work done with a minimum of hassle. Occasionally you might have to turn to another page if the procedure you're working on is accompanied by a *See Also*. That's because there's a lot of overlap among tasks, and we didn't want to keep repeating ourselves. We've scattered some useful *Tips* here and there, pointed out some features that are new in this version of Windows, and thrown in a *Try This* or a *Caution* once in a while. By and large, however, we've tried to remain true to the heart and soul of the book, which is that the information you need should be available to you at a glance.

Useful Tasks...

Whether you use Windows XP on one home computer, on several computers that are part of a home network, or in a home office or small-business environment, we've tried to pack this book with procedures for everything we could think of that you might want to do, from the simplest tasks to some of the more esoteric ones.

...And the Easiest Way to Do Them

Another thing we've tried to do in this book is find and document the easiest way to accomplish a task. Windows XP often provides a multitude of methods to achieve a single end result—which can be daunting or delightful, depending on the way you like to work. If you tend to stick with one favorite and familiar approach, we think the methods described in this book are the way to go. If you like trying out alternative techniques, go ahead! The intuitiveness of Windows XP invites exploration, and you're likely to discover ways of doing things that you think are easier or that you like better than ours. If you do, that's great! It's exactly what the developers of Windows XP had in mind when they provided so many alternatives.

A Quick Overview

Your computer probably came with Windows XP preinstalled, but if you do have to install it yourself, the Setup Wizard makes installation so simple that you won't need our help anyway. So, unlike many computer books, this one doesn't start with installation instructions and a list of system requirements.

Next, you don't have to read this book in any particular order. It's designed so that you can jump in, get the information you need, and then close the book and keep it near your computer. But that doesn't mean we scattered the information about with wild abandon. The tasks you want to accomplish are arranged in two levels. The overall type of task you're looking for is under a main section title such as "Exploring the Internet," "Managing Files and Folders," and so on. Then, in each of those sections, the smaller tasks within the main task are arranged in a loose progression from the simplest to the more complex.

Section 2 covers the basics: starting Windows XP and shutting it down, using the new Fast User Switching feature to change users without having to log off, starting programs and working with program windows, using shortcut menus, taking a class at Mouse School, and getting help if you need it.

Section 3 focuses on running programs, including some of the programs that come with Windows XP. You'll find information here about everyday tasks: composing, editing, saving, opening, and closing documents; copying material between documents; using the Calculator; even what to do if your computer "freezes up." There's a short section here for MS-DOS fans. If you like playing computer games, either by yourself or with other players over the Internet, you'll find the information you need here.

Sections 4 and 5 are all about using Windows XP as your window on the world at large—exploring, communicating, and using some of the tools that let you work and play in cyberspace. We'll help you as you explore the Internet—searching for people and places, finding and revisiting Web sites, designating your home page, viewing Web pages off line, saving and copying material from Web sites, and so on. We'll also talk about communicating with friends and coworkers via e-mail—composing, sending, receiving, and forwarding messages; subscribing to newsgroups; managing and adding to your Contacts list; sending instant messages; and even having online voice and video chats or meetings.

Sections 6 and 7 are all about having fun—working with different types of pictures, including drawings and photographs; scanning pictures; working with pictures from digital or analog cameras and VCRs; assembling slide shows; making great little movies with narration, soundtracks, and fade-in/fade-out transitions between clips; playing and recording CD music; creating and listening to your own music playlist; and trying out Narrator, a program that actually reads aloud to you. The possibilities are endless, and we know you'll be thrilled by the professional results you can achieve with the combination of your own imagination and the Windows XP tools—among them Media Player and Movie Maker—which let you give free rein to your creativity.

Section 8 is the place to go if you have questions about printing your documents or problems setting up your printer. There's a new feature in Windows XP that makes it a snap to print your photographs, and we'll also show you how to print readable Web pages. This section of the book also covers sending, receiving, and annotating faxes, as well as creating useful fax cover pages.

Section 9 covers managing and organizing your documents, files, and folders: moving or copying files, and creating a system of folders in which to keep them; sharing your files with other users; creating quick access to files and folders; recovering deleted items; using compressed folders to minimize large files; storing files on CDs or other types of removable disks; arranging the items on your Desktop; and navigating with toolbars.

Section 10 is all about networking—the different types of networks you're likely to encounter, how to find what you need on your network, and how to use the power of a network to your best advantage. We'll show you, among other things, how to share files and folders, and how to connect to your network in several different ways.

The final sections, 11 through 14, deal with more advanced topics: adding or removing Windows XP components; installing programs; adding hardware; and setting up your printer and your network, as well as setting up dial-up Internet access, Outlook Express, and Fax Service. We'll talk about customizing Windows XP: reverting to the classic Windows look; reorganizing the Start menu; customizing your Desktop, your folder windows, the toolbars, and even the way you enter information, so that everything looks and works exactly the way you want. We'll also discuss improving

your computer's security; protecting your files and folders by specifying who's allowed to access them; protecting your personal information on the Internet; updating your system and maintaining the drives; and diagnosing and fixing problems. These tasks might sound complex, but Windows XP makes them so easy that you'll feel like an expert in no time.

What's New in Windows XP?

Throughout this book you'll see *New Feature* icons identifying features that weren't available in Windows Me (Millennium Edition) or Windows 2000 and that are new in Windows XP. This section, however, might be more aptly entitled "What's New to *You* in Windows XP?" That's because Windows XP has taken the best features from both Windows Me and Windows 2000, improved on them, and added new ones. So, if you've been using Windows Me, you'll find many powerful features that come from Windows 2000 in addition to the completely new features of Windows XP. If you've been using Windows 2000, you'll find that the features incorporated from Windows Me make computing more friendly and more fun. And if you've been using Windows 95 or Windows 98, you'll see all sorts of features that will be completely new to you.

The first thing you'll notice is Windows XP's new interface. This dramatic change isn't merely cosmetic—there are substantial changes to the way Windows functions. For example, Windows detects the content of a folder and then displays the content in the most advantageous view, listing the tasks you can do that apply to that type of content. No more searching around for the right command or window—just click the task you want to accomplish. You'll find that you can customize many items: you can change the look back to that of Windows 2000 if you like, or just change parts of the interface—the Start menu, for example. You can change what the computer does when you insert a music CD or a program CD. You can change the way you log on.

So what's new for *you?* If you've been using the Windows 95/Windows 98/Windows Me family of operating systems, the robustness, security, privacy, and power of Windows XP are new for you. You can use the powerful and secure NTFS disk format to protect your files from prying eyes, even if those eyes belong to other people who use your computer. You'll also be able to use some of the powerful tools of Windows 2000, such as Fax Service to send and receive faxes, and the Computer Management Console to manage just about everything on your computer.

If you're coming from the Windows 2000 and Windows NT family, the friendliness, compatibility, and fun of Windows XP will be new for you. You'll be amazed that you can use so many different types of hardware and software. You can fix problems simply by restoring your computer to an earlier configuration, you can log on easily, and you can customize the system in so many ways. And *yippee*—you can make movies and play games!

You'll find the new Windows XP logon very friendly, and you'll appreciate the new Fast User Switching feature—there's no need to log off when someone else wants to use your computer. Just switch users, and then, when the computer is free, resume work with all your documents and settings intact. If you need to store some files on a CD or make your own music CD, just send the files to your CD recorder, and Windows XP does the rest. The new versions of Internet Explorer, Windows Media Player, and Windows Messenger turn the Internet into your personal service provider—a source of endless information, entertainment, and communication. If you get into trouble, you can ask a friend or colleague for help over the Internet and let him or her take control of your computer and diagnose and fix the problem. And you can avoid any evildoers lurking in cyberspace by installing a firewall that protects your computer from intrusion.

What's new in Windows XP? Perhaps, finally, the feeling that *you* control the computer rather than the computer controlling you!

A Few Assumptions

We had to make a few educated guesses about you, our audience, when we started writing this book. Perhaps your computer is solely for personal use—e-mail, surfing the Internet, playing games, and so on. Perhaps your work allows you to telecommute. Or maybe you run a small home-based business. Taking all these possibilities into account, we assumed either that you'd be using a stand-alone home computer or that you'd have two or more computers connected so that you could share files, a printer, and so on. We also assumed that you had an Internet connection.

Another assumption we made is that—initially, anyway—you'd use Windows XP just as it came, meaning that your folder windows and the Control Panel would show common tasks, and that you'd use your little friend the mouse in the traditional way: that is, point and click to select an item, and then double-click to open it. If you prefer, you can easily set your folder windows not to list common tasks, and you can use the mouse as if you were working on a Web page—pointing to an item to select it and then opening it with a single click. However, because Windows XP's default setup makes accomplishing your work so easy—and because our philosophy is that work should be as stress-free and pleasant as possible—that's what we've used in the procedures and graphics throughout this book.

A Final Word (or Two)

We had three goals in writing this book:

- Whatever you want to do, we want the book to help you get it done.

- We want the book to help you discover how to do things you *didn't* know you wanted to do.

- And, finally, if we've achieved the first two goals, we'll be well on the way to the third, which is for our book to help you *enjoy* using Windows XP. We think that's the best gift we could give you to thank you for buying our book.

We hope you'll have as much fun using *Microsoft Windows XP Plain & Simple* as we've had writing it. The best way to learn is by *doing,* and that's how we hope you'll use this book.

2 Jump Right In

✳ NEW FEATURE

Microsoft Windows XP is designed to work for you, not you for it. Don't be afraid to jump right in and try out some features. You'll find that there are often several ways to accomplish one task. Why? Because people work differently. Because different tasks have different requirements. And because you want to find the way that works best for you, get your work done quickly with a minimum of hassle, and then get away from the computer and live your life!

You'll find that the procedures described in this book are simple and straightforward and that you can often use automated methods to get some of the more complex tasks done easily. This doesn't mean that you can't get stuck or get into trouble, but there are so many safeguards built into Windows XP and so many places where you can get help that you'll have to work pretty hard to get into any *real* trouble.

This section of the book covers the basics: starting Windows XP and shutting it down, starting programs, using Fast User Switching to switch users without having to shut down all your running programs, accessing your documents, arranging your open windows, using the mouse, getting online help, and so on. There's also a handy visual glossary on the following two pages that will help you become familiar with the various components of the Windows XP environment.

Don't change or delete anything just yet—you'll want to feel comfortable with the basics before you do any customizing. The best way to learn about running programs, managing windows, and getting help if you *do* get into trouble is to jump right in and try things out.

What's Where in Windows XP?

Microsoft Windows XP is your working headquarters—the *operating system* that lets you run different programs simultaneously and share information among programs if you need to. Most of the programs you'll use have common characteristics that were designed to work together in the Windows XP environment so that once you learn how to do something in one program, you know how to do it in other programs.

Explorer Bar

Status bar

Title bar

Menu bar

Background picture on the Desktop

A pop-up description of a selected item

Open windows

Start menu

Subfolder (folder inside another folder)

Start button

Similar open windows grouped under one taskbar button

Minimized window of a running program

Take a look at the different parts of the Windows XP environment displayed on these two pages—what they do and what they're called—and you'll be on the road to complete mastery. The way Windows XP was set up on your computer, as well as the many ways in which you can customize Windows XP, can make drastic changes to the look of your Desktop, but the basic concepts are the same. And if you need to, you can always come back to this visual glossary for a quick refresher on Windows XP terminology.

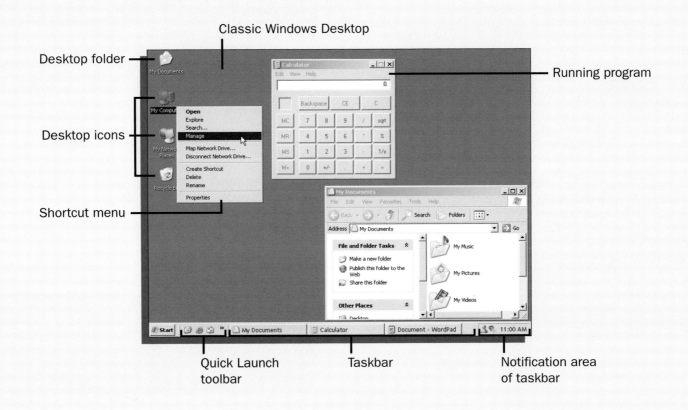

Classic Windows Desktop

Desktop folder

Desktop icons

Shortcut menu

Running program

Quick Launch toolbar

Taskbar

Notification area of taskbar

Starting Up and Shutting Down

When you turn on your computer, you're also starting Windows XP. Startup time depends on your computer's speed, configuration, and connections, and on the programs that are set up to start automatically. When you've finished your work, don't just turn off the computer! Windows XP needs a little time to close any open programs or connections and to save your current settings.

Start Windows XP

1 Turn on your computer, your monitor, and any peripheral devices—your printer, for example.

2 Wait for Windows XP to load.

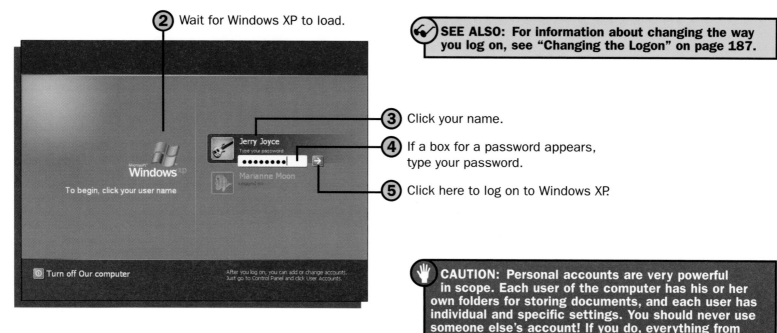

3 Click your name.

4 If a box for a password appears, type your password.

5 Click here to log on to Windows XP.

NEW FEATURE: The Windows Logon and Shut Down options have been simplified, and they list every user who has an account on the computer.

TIP: Your computer can have several states of resting other than simply being turned off. Before you touch the On/Off switch, try pressing a key to see whether the computer comes back to life.

SEE ALSO: For information about changing the way you log on, see "Changing the Logon" on page 187.

CAUTION: Personal accounts are very powerful in scope. Each user of the computer has his or her own folders for storing documents, and each user has individual and specific settings. You should never use someone else's account! If you do, everything from files to e-mail messages could be misplaced or lost.

Shut Down Your Computer

(1) Click the Start button, and then click Turn Off Computer.

(2) Click the appropriate option. The options available depend on the configuration of your computer.

Switches the computer to low-power mode, but your programs are still open. Press any key or move the mouse to reactivate the computer. (On some portable computers, you might have to press the power button.)

Exits Windows XP and then restarts the computer.

Exits Windows XP and prepares the computer to be turned off.

(3) To place the computer in Hibernate mode, hold down the Shift key, and click the Hibernate button when it appears.

Records onto the hard disk all the items contained in the computer's memory, and then shuts down the computer. All the items are restored when you restart the computer.

> **! TIP:** You'll probably want to restart Windows XP after you've made changes to the computer's configuration or if you're having any software problems.

> **SEE ALSO:** For information about logging off and about fast switching of users, see "Switching Users" on page 10.
>
> For information about what to do if you're having problems when you try to quit Windows XP, see "Quitting When You're Stuck" on page 42.

Switching Users ⊕ NEW FEATURE

If someone else wants to log on to your computer and use his or her own settings, you have two choices: you can log off and thereby close all the programs and network connections you were using, or you can simply switch users. Switching users is obviously a great idea! You can leave all your programs running, and as soon as the other person has finished with the computer, you can get back to work and find everything just as it was before you switched users.

> ✋ **CAUTION:** Leaving your programs running uses some of the computer's resources, so the other person who's using the computer might find that it's running slowly. If you notice that the computer's performance has degraded when you use fast switching, log off to free up those resources.

Change Users

① Click the Start button, and click Log Off to display the Log Off Windows dialog box.

② Click the action you want:

- Switch User to suspend your use of the computer and allow someone else to log on to the computer and immediately be able to use his or her own Desktop configurations and other settings

- Log Off to close all your running programs, save your settings, and sign yourself off the computer

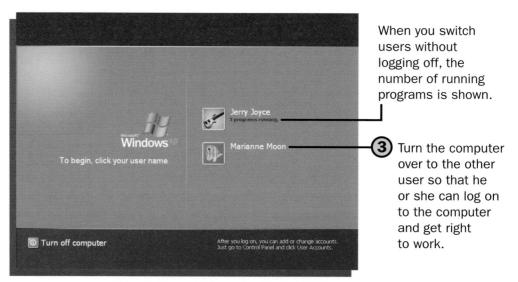

When you switch users without logging off, the number of running programs is shown.

③ Turn the computer over to the other user so that he or she can log on to the computer and get right to work.

Starting a Program

The real work of an operating system is to run software programs. Windows XP comes with a wide variety of programs, and you can install additional (and often more powerful) ones. Most programs are listed on the Start menu, but Windows XP gives you several ways to start your programs, so you can choose the way that's easiest for you or the one you like best.

Start a Program

(1) Do any of the following:

- Click the Start button, and choose a program from the Start menu.

- Click the Start button, point to All Programs, point to any relevant program groups to display additional submenus, and choose the program you want.

- Point to and then double-click the program icon on the Desktop.

- Open the My Computer folder, navigate to the folder that contains the program you want, and double-click the program.

- Open the My Computer folder, navigate to the folder that contains a file associated with the program, and double-click the file.

- Insert the CD that contains a program that's designed to run from the CD, and choose to run the program.

- Click the Start button, choose Run, type the full path and file name of the program, and click OK.

(2) Use the program, and close it when you've finished.

> **(!) TIP:** The programs listed in the table at the right are only some of the programs that come with Windows XP. You'll find descriptions of some of the other programs elsewhere in this book.

Frequently Used Windows XP Programs

Program	Purpose
Address Book	Stores names, addresses, and other contact information.
Calculator	Does arithmetic calculations and complex mathematical calculations.
Character Map	Inserts special characters from installed fonts.
Internet Explorer	Functions as a Web browser and an HTML document viewer.
Magnifier	Magnifies sections of the screen.
MSN Explorer	Provides a customized Web browser that works easily with MSN Web sites.
Narrator	Describes and reads aloud the screen contents.
Notepad	Creates, edits, and displays text documents.
On-Screen Keyboard	Allows keyboard input using the mouse or other pointing device.
Outlook Express	Provides e-mail, newsgroup, and directory services.
Paint	Creates and edits bitmap pictures; imports and edits scanned images and digital pictures.
Sound Recorder	Creates and plays digital sound files.
Windows Media Player	Plays sound, music, and video.
Windows Movie Maker	Converts, edits, organizes, and distributes audio and video files.
WordPad	Creates, edits, and displays text, Rich Text Format, and Word documents.

Accessing Your Documents

The My Documents folder is a personal storage area where you can keep and access your documents. The My Computer folder is the gateway to your computer's contents, and it displays the icons that represent all your local storage areas: removable disk drives, hard disks, CD drives, and so on. From here you can venture as deep into the folder structure of your computer as you dare.

> **NEW FEATURE:** The My Documents folder, the My Computer icon, and a few other familiar icons that appeared on the Desktop in earlier versions of Windows might or might not be on your Desktop, depending on whether Windows XP was installed on a new computer or was upgraded from a previous version of Windows. You can change the settings to hide or display the icons.

Open My Documents

(1) Click the Start button, and choose My Documents from the Start menu to open the My Documents window.

(2) Click a file to select it.

(3) Read about the tasks you can do with this file.

(4) Click to see the details about the file.

(5) Double-click a file to open it.

(7) Click the Close button when you've finished.

Scroll box

(6) Use the scroll bars, if necessary, to view all the documents. Click the scroll arrows to scroll a small increment at a time, or drag the scroll box to scroll a greater distance.

Scroll arrow

> **TIP:** If you can't find the file you need in the My Documents folder, click a different location in the Other Places section of the window.

> **TIP:** Each user of the computer (provided he or she logs on) has a separate My Documents folder, as well as other personalized settings. The My Documents folder is quickly accessible from the Start menu, but it's actually located in the Documents And Settings folder under the user's name.

Open Any Folder

1 Click the Start button, and choose My Computer from the Start menu to open the My Computer window.

3 Read the information about the drive and the actions you can take.

SEE ALSO: For information about changing the way folders are displayed, see "Changing the Window View" on page 129 and "Windows Views" on page 130.

2 Click a drive icon to select it.

4 Double-click the drive icon to open a window for that drive.

9 Click the Close button when you've finished.

5 Click the Back button to return to the previous window, the Forward button to move to a previously visited subfolder, or the Up button to move from a subfolder back to its parent folder.

8 To open a folder, double-click it.

6 Select a folder or a file, and read about the tasks you can do with this folder or file.

7 Click a new destination if you want to work in a different folder.

Switching Among Open Windows

Whatever your working style, it's inevitable that you'll end up with more than one window open on your computer—your My Documents window and your My Network Places window, perhaps, or a couple of program windows. Instead of closing one window to get to another, you can simply switch windows.

Select a Window

NEW FEATURE: If there isn't enough room on the taskbar to display a button for each open window, Windows XP groups similar types of windows under one button. To arrange all the windows in the group, right-click the button, and choose the arrangement you want from the shortcut menu that appears.

(1) On the taskbar, click to switch to the window you want.

(2) If Windows XP has grouped similar types of windows, click the button for the grouping, and then click the window you want.

(3) Click the name of the window to open the window.

TRY THIS: Hold down the Alt key and press the Tab key. Still holding down the Alt key, press the Tab key several times. Note that the selection cycles through all the open windows. When you release the Alt key, you switch to the window that was selected.

Mouse Maneuvers

Navigating with a mouse is like traveling in a helicopter: you can lift off from any spot and set down wherever you want. Using the keyboard is like taking the scenic route—you get to explore the road less traveled, and you might even come across features and techniques that are new to you. But to finish your tasks as quickly as possible—and to take advantage of some of the best features of Windows XP—give your mouse the job!

Before you fly off on your mouse wings, you might need some Mouse Basics. Here at Mouse School you'll learn to point, click, double-click, right-click, select, multiple-select, and drag with your mouse. Don't be too surprised if the mouse acts a bit differently from the way you expect it to. Windows XP gives you numerous options for customizing the way your mouse works, so be patient and experiment a bit. And read "Customizing Your Folders" on page 188 for information about setting up Windows XP so that your mouse works the way you want it to.

Point: Move the mouse until the mouse pointer (either a small arrow-shaped pointer or a tiny hand) is pointing to the item you want.

 Depending on your mouse-click settings, either you click an item to select it...

...or the item becomes selected when you simply point to it.

Click: Point to the item you want, and then quickly press down and release the left mouse button.

Double-click: Point to the item you want, and then quickly press down and release the left mouse button twice, being careful not to move the mouse between clicks.

Right-click: Point to the item you want, and then quickly press down and release the right mouse button.

Select: Point to an item, and click to select it. To select an icon when the system is set to open an item with a single click, point to the icon but don't click. A selected item is usually a different color from other similar items or is surrounded by a frame.

Multiple-select: To select a list of adjacent or sequential items, click the first item, hold down the Shift key, and click the last item. To select or deselect *nonadjacent* items, hold down the Ctrl key and click each item you want. (Not all windows and dialog boxes permit multiple selection.)

Drag: Select the item you want. Keeping the mouse pointer on the selected item, hold down the left mouse button and move the mouse until you've "dragged" the item to the desired location; then release the left mouse button.

Point to the item...

...and drag it into a new location.

Managing Windows

"Managing" a window means bossing it around: you can move it, change its size, and open and close it. Most programs are contained in windows. Although these windows might have some different features, most program windows have more similarities than differences.

! TIP: To automatically arrange all the windows on your Desktop, right-click a blank spot on the taskbar, and choose the arrangement you want from the shortcut menu.

Use the Buttons to Switch Between Sizes

The program's title bar — Buttons for switching between window sizes

TRY THIS: Double-click the title bar of a maximized window to restore the window to its original size. Double-click the title bar again to return the window to its maximized size. Now press Alt+Spacebar to open the window's Control menu, and choose the action you want from the menu.

1 Click the Maximize button, and the window enlarges and fills the screen. (If the window is already maximized, you won't see the Maximize button.)

2 Click the Restore Down button, and the window gets smaller. (If the window is already restored, you won't see the Restore Down button.)

3 Click the Minimize button, and the window disappears but you can see its name on a button on the taskbar.

4 Click the window's name on the taskbar button, and the window zooms back to the size it was before you minimized it.

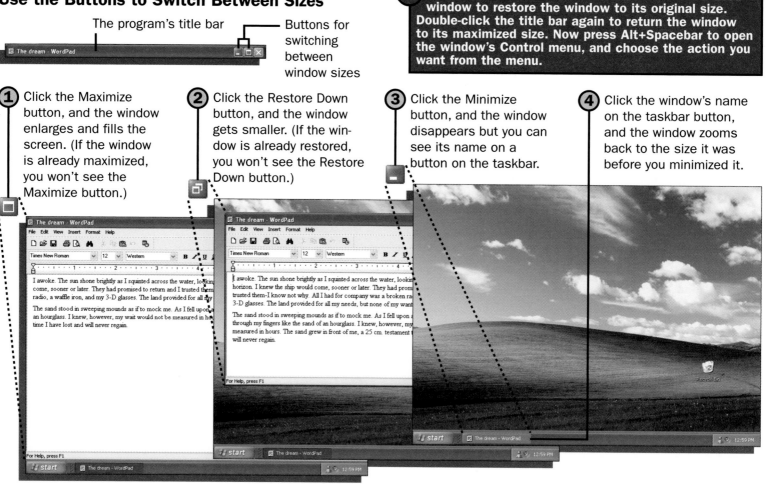

Use the Mouse to Resize a Window

1 Move the mouse over one of the borders of the window until the mouse pointer changes into a two-headed arrow. Drag the window border until the window is the size you want. The directions of the arrowheads show you the directions in which you can move the window border.

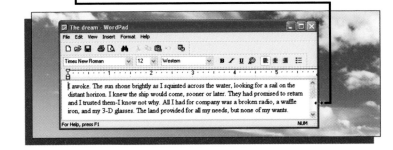

Move a Window

1 Point to the window's title bar.

2 Drag the window to a new location.

! TIP: Move your mouse over a side border to change the window's width, over a top or bottom border to change the window's height, and over a corner to change both height and width.

! TIP: To see the contents of a window when you move it rather than seeing a blank placeholder rectangle, right-click the Desktop, choose Properties from the shortcut menu, and, on the Effects tab, select the Show Window Contents While Dragging check box.

⊙ SEE ALSO: For information about dragging items with the mouse, see "Mouse Maneuvers" on page 15.

! TIP: You can't manually resize a maximized window, so if the window you want to resize is currently maximized, click the Restore Down button.

Getting Help

What are big and colorful; packed with information, procedures, shortcuts, and links to online information; and sadly underutilized? The Help programs! Of course, they couldn't possibly replace this book, but you can use them to find concise step-by-step procedures for diagnosing and overcoming problems, and to explore many aspects of managing Windows XP. There are three basic types of help: the Help And Support Center, Program Help, and dialog box Help.

Use the Help And Support Center

① Click the Start button, and choose Help And Support to open the Help And Support Center.

② Click a link to the main topic of interest. If the item has subtopics, click the subtopic you want.

> **⚠ TIP: Once you've found the information you want to read as you step through procedures, click the Change View button to display only the relevant information and hide all the extra material.**

④ If you can't find the information you need, type a word or phrase, and press Enter. If your search is unproductive, click Set Search Options, change what's to be searched for, and try again.

⑥ To look up another topic, click Home to return to the main page.

⑤ If you still can't find the information, connect to the Internet, and click Support to use resources on the Internet.

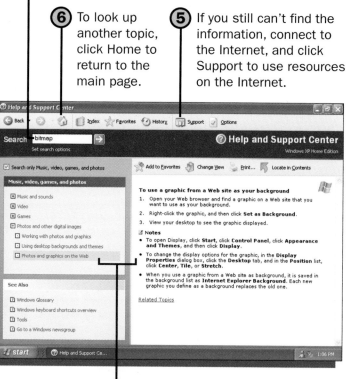

③ If additional links are displayed, click the link that best suits your needs, and then read the information.

Use Program Help

1 Choose Help Topics from the program's Help menu to open the Help program.

4 If you can't find the information you need, click the Index tab, and search for help using keywords.

5 Click the Close button when you've finished.

2 On the Contents tab, click the main topic of interest. Click a subtopic if necessary.

3 Read the information.

Use Dialog Box Help

1 In any Windows XP dialog box, click the Help button.

3 Read the Help information, and then click anywhere to close Help.

2 Click the item you want information about.

SEE ALSO: For information about getting online help from someone you hope will be knowledgeable about computers and programs, see "Helping Each Other" on page 226.

TIP: To get a printed copy of a Help topic, click Print. To copy information, select the text, and press Ctrl+C. You can then press Ctrl+V to paste the copied text into a program such as WordPad.

Using Shortcut Menus for Quick Results

Windows XP and the programs that work with it were designed to be intuitive—that is, they anticipate what you're likely to want to do when you're working on a particular task, and they place the appropriate commands on a shortcut menu that you open by clicking the *right* mouse button. These shortcut menus are *dynamic,* which means they change depending on the task in progress.

Use a Shortcut Menu Command

① Right-click an item.

TRY THIS: See what's on the shortcut menus. Right-click the Start button, and note the commands on the shortcut menu that appears. Now right-click a button on the taskbar, and then right-click a blank spot on the taskbar. Open the Start menu and right-click an item. Continue experimenting by right-clicking the Recycle Bin icon on the Desktop, other items on the Desktop, and various files and folders in folder windows. Amazing, isn't it?

② Choose a command from the shortcut menu to accomplish the task at hand. If the item or action you want isn't on the shortcut menu, do any of the following:

● From the shortcut menu, choose any items whose names have arrows next to them to see whether the item or action you want is on one of the shortcut menu's submenus.

● Check to be sure that you right-clicked the proper item.

● Check the program's documentation or help files to verify that what you want to do can be accomplished from the item you right-clicked.

NEW FEATURE: The tasks listed in a folder window are also dynamic, depending on the types of files in the folder, but they usually provide actions that are less specific than those listed on a shortcut menu.

TIP: If you're not sure how to accomplish what you want to do, right-click the item in question, and you'll usually see an appropriate command on the shortcut menu.

3 Running Programs and Playing Games

Getting to know the programs that come with Microsoft Windows XP is a bit like moving into new living quarters. Just as your new abode has the basics—stove, refrigerator, and (dare we say it?) windows—the Windows XP operating system comes with many basic accessories and tools. Just as you'll add all the accoutrements that transform empty rooms into a cozy home, you'll add programs to Windows XP to utilize its full potential as you work (and play).

But let's cover the basics first. There's WordPad, a handy little word processor; and Calculator, for scientific calculations as well as quick basic arithmetic. In this section, we'll concentrate on some everyday tasks: composing, saving, and printing a document; creating and editing text; copying items between documents that were created in different programs; and inserting characters such as © and é that don't exist on your keyboard. We'll also take a look at the Calculator and try out some different types of calculations. Finally, we'll discuss working at the command prompt, running MS-DOS programs, and what you can do to get out of trouble when a program isn't working properly.

This section wouldn't be complete without some information about the games that come with Windows XP. Whether you want to take a few minutes to work off some energy with a quick game of Pinball, lose yourself for an hour in a game of Solitaire, or go further afield and seek out players from around the world to join you in an international game of Backgammon or Checkers, Windows is ready to play!

Composing a Document

WordPad is a powerful little word processor with which you can create documents in Rich Text format, or as plain text or Unicode text documents. In most cases you'll want to create a document with formatting for a well-designed, professional look. Save the document as you create it, and print it when you've finished.

Create a Document

(1) Start WordPad from the Accessories submenu of the Start menu. If WordPad is already running, click the New button on the toolbar, click Rich Text Document in the list, and click OK.

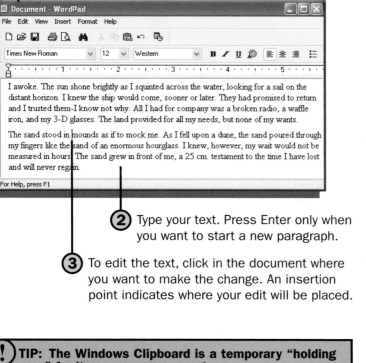

(2) Type your text. Press Enter only when you want to start a new paragraph.

(3) To edit the text, click in the document where you want to make the change. An insertion point indicates where your edit will be placed.

> **⚠ TIP: The Windows Clipboard is a temporary "holding area" for items you copy or cut.**

I awoke. The sun shone brightly as I squinted across the water, looking for a sail on the distant horizon. I knew the ship would come, sooner or later. They had promised to return and I trusted them-I know not why. All I had for company was a broken radio, a waffle iron, and my 3-D glasses. The land provided for all my needs, but none of my wants.

The sand stood in sweeping mounds as if to mock me. As I fell upon a dune, the sand poured through my fingers like the sand of an enormous hourglass. I knew, however, my wait would not be measured in hours. The sand grew in front of me, a 25 cm. testament to the time I have lost and will never regain.

(4) To insert additional text into a paragraph you've already typed, click where you want to insert the new text, and type it. If the text you want to insert is stored on the Clipboard, click the Paste button on the toolbar instead of typing the text.

I awoke. The sun shone brightly as I squinted across the water, looking for a sail on the distant horizon. I knew the ship would come, sooner or later. They had promised to return and I trusted them-I know not why. All I had for company was a broken radio, a waffle iron, and my 3-D glasses. The land provided for all my needs, but none of my wants.

The sand stood in sweeping mounds as if to mock me. As I fell upon a dune, the sand poured through my fingers like the sand of an enormous hourglass. I knew, however, my wait would not be measured in hours. The sand grew in front of me, a 25 cm. testament to the time I have lost and will never regain.

(5) To delete text, select it, and press Delete. To save the text for later use instead of deleting it, place it on the Clipboard by clicking the Cut button on the toolbar.

I awoke. The sun shone brightly as I squinted across the water, looking for a sail on the distant horizon. I knew the ship would come, sooner or later. They had promised to return and I trusted them-I know not why. All I had for company was a broken radio, a waffle iron, and my 3-D glasses. The land provided for all my needs, but none of my wants.

The sand stood in sweeping mounds as if to mock me. As I fell upon a dune, the sand poured through my fingers like the sand of an hourglass. I knew, however, my wait would not be measured in hours. The sand grew in front of me, a 25 cm. testament to the time I have lost and will never regain.

(6) To replace existing text with different text, select the text, and then type the new text.

Format the Document

① Select the text to be formatted.

② Specify the font, font size, and font script (the locale or type of font). Apply bold, italic, underlined, or color emphasis as desired.

③ Click in the paragraph you want to format, or select all the paragraphs to which you want to apply the same formatting.

④ Use the Alignment buttons to align your text, or use the Bullets button to create a bulleted list.

CAUTION: If you're planning to save your document as a Text Document (plain text), don't apply any formatting to it. If you do, all the formatting will be lost when you save the document.

TRY THIS: Select some text in a document, and choose Font from the Format menu. In the Font dialog box, specify a font, a font size, and any emphasis you want, and click OK. Now click in a paragraph, choose Paragraph from the Format menu, and use the Paragraph dialog box to set exact measurements for the paragraph indents you want. Click OK. Choose Tabs from the Format menu, and use the Tabs dialog box to set the exact position of any tabs you want in the paragraph. Click OK. Now move to the end of the paragraph, press Enter, and type some text. You'll see that all the paragraph formatting from the previous paragraph has been copied and applied to the new paragraph.

⑤ Drag the indent markers to set the left, right, and first-line indents. Click in the ruler to set a tab stop.

⑥ Save the document.

Saving, Closing, and Opening a Document

After you've created a document, you'll probably want to save it for later use. When you've finished using the program in which you created the document, close the program so that it isn't using space or taking power from your computer. Then, when you're ready to work on your document again, you can easily restart the program and open the document directly from the running program.

Save a Document

1 Click the Save button on the toolbar, or, if the toolbar isn't visible, choose Save from the File menu.

2 If you don't want to save the document to the default folder, specify a different drive or folder.

6 As you work with the document, click Save frequently. Windows will now save the file without displaying the Save As dialog box.

5 Click Save.

TIP: In many programs, you can press Ctrl+S to quickly save a document.

Close a Document

1 Click the Save button one last time to make sure that you've saved all changes in the document.

2 Click the Close button to end the program.

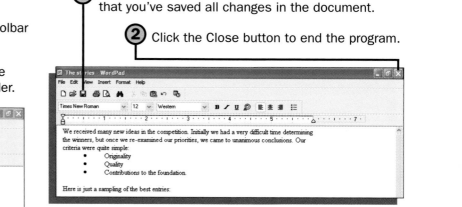

3 Type a name for the document. The name can be up to 255 characters long; it can contain spaces but can't contain the * : < > | " \ or /characters.

4 If you want to save the document in a different format from that of the default file format, select the format.

CAUTION: Long file names are often truncated by programs, so a descriptive short name is better than a long one. If you want to include the full path to a file, you can use the : and \ characters in the File Name box.

Open a Document

① With the program you want to use running, choose Open from the File menu to display the Open dialog box.

Click to browse through the drives and folders of the computer and the network to specify a location.

Click to see a list of documents and folders you've used recently.

② If necessary, specify the location of the document.

③ If necessary, double-click a folder to navigate to the document. Continue double-clicking folders until you locate the document.

④ Specify the file type of the document you want to open. Only documents of the specified file type will be displayed in the list of files.

⑤ Double-click the document to open it.

TRY THIS: Many programs can stay open for additional work even after you close the document you're working on. Open the File menu and look at the commands. If there's a Close command, click it to close the document without closing the program. If there's a New command but no Close command, choose New to see whether it closes the open document.

TIP: Most, but not all, programs use the Save As and Open dialog boxes just like the ones used by WordPad. If you have a program that uses its own style of dialog box, you'll probably need to consult the program's documentation if you need additional help.

Copying Material Between Documents

It's easy to copy material from a document that was created in one program to a document that was created in another program. The way you insert the material depends on what it is. If it's similar to and compatible with the receiving document—text that's being copied into a Microsoft Word document, for example—you can usually insert it as is and can edit it in the receiving document's program. If the item is dissimilar—a sound clip, say, inserted into a Word document—either it's *encapsulated,* or isolated, as an object and can be edited in the originating program only, or you simply are not able to paste that item into your document.

Copy and Insert Material

(1) In the source document, select the material you want to copy.

(2) Choose Copy from the Edit menu. Windows places copied items on the Windows Clipboard. (You can copy only one item at a time, so always paste the Clipboard contents into your document before you copy anything else, or you'll lose whatever was on the Clipboard.)

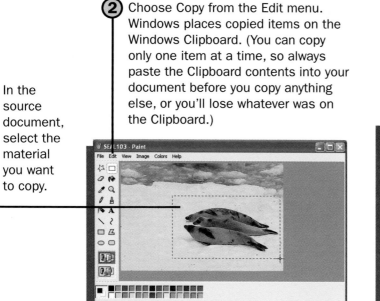

(3) Switch to the destination document.

(4) Click where you want to insert the material.

(5) Click the Paste button or choose Paste from the Edit menu.

!TIP: To insert the copied material in a different format, or as an icon for an online document, choose Paste Special from the Edit menu instead of the Paste command.

!TIP: Some programs—those that are part of Microsoft Office, for example—have their own Clipboard, which allows you to store and retrieve multiple copied items from Office programs.

Dialog Box Decisions

You're going to be seeing a lot of *dialog boxes* as you use Windows XP, and if you're not familiar with them now, you soon will be. Dialog boxes appear when Windows XP or a program—WordPad, let's say—needs you to make one or more decisions about what you want to do. Sometimes all you have to do is click a Yes, a No, or an OK button; at other times, there'll be quite a few decisions to make in one dialog box. The Print dialog box, shown below, is typical of many dialog boxes and is one you'll probably be seeing frequently, so take a look at its components and the way they work.

Title bar; drag it to move the dialog box.

Click to select an item.

Select a check box to turn on an option. Clear the check box to turn off the option.

Click an option button to turn on one option in the group.

Click the Close button to close the dialog box.

Click the Help button, and then click an item in the dialog box for information about that item.

Click to open a different dialog box to see more choices.

Click to increase or decrease a value.

Click to apply your choices and leave the dialog box open for more changes.

An option that's grayed is currently unavailable.

Type information into a text box.

Click to cancel your decisions and close the dialog box.

Click to put your decisions into effect—in this case, to print your document.

Print

General

Select Printer

Add Printer HP LaserJet 4/4M PS ...

Status: Ready
Location:
Comment:

Print to file   Preferences
Find Printer...

Page Range
- All
- Selection   Current Page
- Pages: 1-65535

Enter either a single page number or a single page range. For example, 5-12

Number of copies: 1

Collate

Print   Cancel   Apply

Inserting Special Characters

Windows XP provides a special accessory program called Character Map that lets you insert into your programs the characters and symbols that aren't available on your keyboard. Character Map displays all the characters that are available for each of the fonts on your computer.

Find and Insert a Character

(1) Start Character Map from the System Tools submenu of the Start menu.

(2) Specify a font.

Select this check box to use search features to locate a character.

Displays the characters you've selected to be copied to the Clipboard.

(3) Double-click the character you want to insert. Double-click any other characters that you want to insert at the same time.

(4) Click Copy to place the character or characters on the Clipboard.

Here are some currency symbols you might encounter on your trip:
£ Pts €

(5) Switch to your program, click where you want to insert the character or characters, and press Ctrl+V (or choose Paste from the Edit menu) to paste the character or characters from the Clipboard into your document. Format and edit the inserted text as desired.

CAUTION: The Windows Clipboard is a temporary "holding area" for items you want to cut or copy and paste. The Clipboard can hold only one item at a time, so do your pasting immediately after you've done your copying.

TIP: Click a character to see an enlarged view of it to ensure that you're selecting the correct character.

TRY THIS: In Character Map, select a character you insert frequently, and note the keyboard shortcut for the character in the bottom right corner of the Character Map dialog box. Switch to the program into which you want to insert the character, hold down the Alt key, and use the numeric keypad to enter the numbers. Format the inserted character with a different font or font size if desired.

Crunching Numbers

Need to do a quick calculation but don't have enough fingers? Want to convert a decimal number into a hexadecimal or binary number? You can do these procedures, and even a few complex geometric and statistical calculations, with the Calculator.

Use the Calculator

(1) Start the Calculator from the Accessories submenu of the Start menu.

(2) Either click the number buttons or type the numerals you want. Continue until you've entered the entire number.

(3) Click a function.

(4) Enter the next number.

(5) When you've entered all the numbers, click the equal (=) button. Press Ctrl+C to copy the result if you want to paste it into your document.

> **! TIP: To speed up your calculations, use the numeric keypad on your computer's keyboard, pressing the + − * / and Enter keys instead of clicking the corresponding buttons. Make sure, however, that the Num Lock key is turned on.**

> **! TIP: To determine the purpose of a key and to view its keyboard shortcut, right-click the key, and choose What's This? from the shortcut menu.**

Make Complex Calculations

(1) Choose Scientific from the View menu.

(2) Choose a numbering system if you don't want to calculate using the standard decimal system.

(3) Enter a value.

(4) Use any of the function keys to calculate a new value.

Running Commands

In Windows XP, the command prompt is the place where you can execute *command-line* instructions. Most of the commands are the old standard MS-DOS commands, some are enhancements of the MS-DOS commands, and others are commands that are unique to Windows XP. When you want or need to work from the command prompt, you can open a command prompt window and execute all your tasks there, including using the basic commands, starting a program, and even starting a program in a new window.

Run a Command

① Open a command prompt window by choosing Command Prompt from the Accessories submenu of the Start menu.

② At the prompt, type a command, including any *switches* and extra *parameters,* and press Enter.

③ Enter any additional commands you want to run.

```
Command Prompt                                    _ □ x
C:\Accounting>cd ..
C:\>prompt $T $P$G
13:58:34.66 C:\>a:
13:58:44.82 A:\>dir
 Volume in drive A has no label.
 Volume Serial Number is 14D1-C60D

 Directory of A:\

06/28/2001  05:46 PM           176,369 Mountain.JPG
               1 File(s)        176,369 bytes
               0 Dir(s)       1,281,024 bytes free
13:58:46.53 A:\>c:
13:58:55.54 C:\>cd windows
13:59:07.59 C:\WINDOWS>cd \
13:59:16.85 C:\>cls_
```

> ✋ **CAUTION:** The command prompt is a powerful weapon that can disrupt your system, delete files, and create general havoc. Don't execute commands unless you know what they're designed for.

> ⓘ **TIP:** Many commands have switches that allow the use of extra parameters, giving you greater control of the command. A switch is the part of the command with the forward slash (/), followed by a letter, a number, or another instruction. A parameter is an additional instruction you provide, such as the file name or drive letter.

The Top 10 Command Prompt Commands

Command	Function
cd	Switches to the specified folder (or directory).
cls	Clears the screen.
copy	Copies the specified files or folders.
dir	Shows the contents of the current directory.
drive:	Switches to the specified drive (type the drive letter and a colon).
exit	Ends the session.
mem	Displays memory configuration.
path	Displays or sets the path the command searches.
prompt	Changes the information displayed at the prompt.
rename	Renames the specified file or files if the wildcard characters ? or * are used.

Find a Command

1 At the command prompt, type **help** and press Enter.

2 Review the list of commands.

3 If the information scrolls off the screen, use the scroll bar or the scroll arrows so that you can see the entire list.

Get Information About a Command

1 Type a command followed by a space and **/?** and then press Enter to get information about the command.

2 Read the information.

3 If the information scrolls off the screen, use the scroll bar or the scroll arrows so that you can see the entire text.

> **! TIP:** To change some of the settings for the command prompt window—the font, the cursor size, or the colors, for example—right-click the window's title bar, and choose Properties from the shortcut menu.

> **TRY THIS:** At the command prompt, type help > dosref.txt and press Enter. Now use Notepad or WordPad to open the file *dosref.txt* that's stored on your hard disk (it's the folder that was active when you typed the command). The > symbol redirected the output from the screen to the file. You now have a reference for the commands, which you can easily print out.

Playing FreeCell

FreeCell—a modified version of Solitaire—is a game you play by yourself. The entire deck is dealt, and, as in Solitaire, you arrange the cards by stacking them in descending order, alternating the red and black cards. Unlike the way you play Solitaire, the sequence of cards can begin anywhere in the stack. You can move a single card onto another card to add to the sequence of cards, or into one of the free cells at the top, or into a blank column after the column has been emptied of cards. You win by stacking all the cards by suit in ascending order.

> **TIP:** If there are enough available free cells, you can move an entire series of cards from one column into another.

> **TIP:** Try to free the Ace cards early in the game and to keep as many free cells and empty columns as possible.

Play FreeCell

1 Start FreeCell from the Games submenu of the Start menu.

Free cells —

2 When possible, move an Ace to the top of the window and stack the cards by suit in ascending order (FreeCell might do this for you automatically).

3 Click to select the card you want to move.

4 Click another card to move the selected card on top of it. (The cards must be stacked in alternating colors in descending numeric order.)

5 Continue stacking the cards, including moving cards into or from a free cell. You can also move one card or a series of cards into an empty column.

6 Repeat steps 2 through 5 until all the cards are stacked by suit.

Playing Hearts

You play Hearts against three hands controlled by the computer. The objective is to score the *fewest* points. For each trick you win, you're awarded one point for each heart and 13 points for the Queen of Spades. You must use the same suit that's played first unless you're void of that suit. You take the trick if you've played the highest card of the suit played.

Play Hearts

① Start Hearts from the Games submenu of the Start menu.

② Enter your playing name, and click OK.

> **!** TIP: To play against real people rather than against the computer, choose Internet Hearts from the Games submenu.

> **!** TIP: Another scoring option is to "shoot the moon," whereby you collect all the points in one hand. If you succeed, each of the other players receives 26 points, and you receive zero points for the hand.

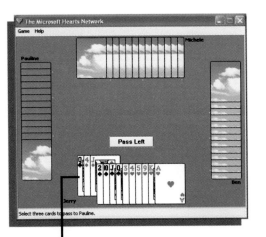

③ Click the cards to be passed, and click the Pass button. Click the OK button after you've received your cards.

④ The Two of Clubs is automatically played to start the game. If you don't have the Two of Clubs, wait for your turn, and then click the card you want to play. Continue playing until the first player scores 100 or more points. The lowest score wins.

Playing Minesweeper

Minesweeper is a game you play against the computer. The goal is to uncover, in the shortest possible time, all the squares that don't contain mines. If you uncover a square that contains a mine, you lose. The key is to use the numbers in the uncovered squares to determine which adjacent squares contain the mines.

> ⚠️ **TIP: The number in a square represents the total number of mines in adjacent squares—directly above, below, diagonal to, or to the left or right of the numbered square. Use several exposed numbers to figure out where the mines are.**

Play Minesweeper

1 Start Minesweeper from the Games submenu of the Start menu.

Number of mines left

Elapsed time

2 Click a square to uncover it. You might need to click more squares before you can use the numbers of adjacent mines to determine mine locations.

4 Click a square that you believe doesn't contain a mine. Continue finding unmined squares and marking squares that contain mines until you've revealed all the unmined squares.

3 Right-click to mark a square that you believe contains a mine. If you're not sure, right-click the square a second time to mark it as a possible mine.

> ⚠️ **TIP: If the game is too easy or too difficult, choose a different level of difficulty for the game from the Game menu. The greater the level of difficulty, the more squares and mines the game contains.**

Playing Pinball

Pinball is a dazzling game with extensive sound effects. The object of the game is to keep each ball in play as long as possible while scoring the greatest number of points. Unlike most computer games, Pinball is played using the keyboard exclusively. You have three balls for the game unless you win extra balls, and you can advance through nine steps, or ranks, with each rank being more difficult to achieve and awarding a greater number of points.

> ✋ **CAUTION: Use the Nudge keys sparingly and very cautiously—it's quite easy to tilt the game.**

Play Pinball

(1) Start Pinball from the Games submenu of the Start menu.

(2) On the Options menu, specify how many players are in the game.

(3) Hold down the Spacebar and then release it to shoot the ball into play.

(4) Use the keys as shown in the table to control the play.

Pinball Control Keys

Key	Function
Z	Left flipper and reentry lane lights
/ (forward slash)	Right flipper
X	Nudge from left
. (period)	Nudge from right
Up arrow key	Nudge from bottom
F2	New game
F3	Pause/resume
F4	Full screen/window

> ❗ **TIP: Press the F8 key to change which keys you want to use to control the game.**

> ❗ **TIP: Pressing either flipper button changes which reentry lanes are lit.**

Playing Solitaire

Solitaire is a classic card game that, as its name implies, you play by yourself. The object is to reveal all the cards that are turned face down and eventually to arrange all the cards in four piles, with each pile being a single suit stacked in ascending order from Ace through King.

TIP: To change the way a game is played, choose Options from the Game menu. To change the pattern of the card backs, choose Deck from the Game menu.

Play Solitaire

(1) Start Solitaire from the Games submenu of the Start menu.

(2) Use the mouse to drag one card on top of another card. (The cards must be stacked in descending numeric order, alternating the red and black cards.)

(5) When you can't make a play, click the stack of cards to turn the cards over. Drag the top card on top of a face-up card if the top card has the correct number and suit.

(3) Drag any Ace cards into the top row. If there are any other cards for that suit in the pile, stack them in ascending numeric order.

(4) If one or more face-up cards are moved to expose a face-down card, click the face-down card to display its face.

(6) If all the cards have been moved from a row, move a King, if one is available, and any cards that are stacked on it, into the empty spot.

TIP: Microsoft Plus! For Windows XP includes three more games—HyperBowl, Russian Square, and Labyrinth—that you can install on your computer.

Playing Spider Solitaire

Spider Solitaire is yet another version of Solitaire. Unlike the way you play other Solitaire games, the object is to stack the cards by suit in one column in descending order. When a series from King to Ace is complete, the cards are removed. The level of difficulty is determined by how many suits are used (one, two, or four).

Play Spider Solitaire

TIP: To display possible moves, press the M key. Press it again to see another possible move.

TIP: Choose Save This Game from the Game menu to save the game for later play.

(1) Start Spider Solitaire from the Games submenu of the Start menu.

(3) Use the mouse to drag one card on top of another card. You can stack the cards in descending numeric order regardless of suit, but it's best to stack by suit.

Difficulty

Select the game difficulty level that you want:

♠ ◉ Easy: One Suit
♥ ♠ ○ Medium: Two Suits
♦ ♠ ♥ ♠ ○ Difficult: Four Suits

OK   Cancel

(2) Specify how many suits you want to use.

(4) Drag a group of sequential cards of the same suit onto another card. (Only cards of the same suit can be moved as a group.)

(6) If no moves are available, click the stacked cards to deal another round. (You can't deal if there's an empty column.) Continue playing until all the cards have been removed or until all the cards have been dealt and there are no longer any moves available.

(5) If there's an empty column, move a card or a sequence of cards into the column.

Playing Games Over the Internet

Windows XP provides five games—Backgammon, Checkers, Hearts, Reversi, and Spades—that are designed to be played against other players over the Internet. When you start a game and connect to the Internet, the game server will try to find players matched to your skill level and language. (You can't select the players or the locations of your opponents.) You can communicate with the other players by using the Chat feature.

!TIP: To play additional types of games and to select specific individuals to be your opponents, connect to the Gaming Zone. You'll see the MSN Gaming Zone item on the Contents tab of the Help program in the game you're currently playing.

Play a Game

1 Start an Internet game from the Games submenu of the Start menu.

5 At the conclusion of the game, use the Game menu to start a new game with the same players, to start a game with different players, or to quit playing.

3 Click a message to send to your opponent.

2 Click Play. If you're not already connected to the Internet, connect when prompted.

4 Play the game and make your moves as prompted.

!TIP: You can also play certain games over the Internet using Windows Messenger, provided you and your opponent both have the games installed.

SEE ALSO: For information about playing games over the Internet using Windows Messenger, see "Sending Instant Messages" on page 68.

Running Older Programs

Most programs work well with Windows XP. Some older ones, however, are designed exclusively for earlier versions of Windows, and don't work properly in Windows XP. However, Windows XP can get those programs to run by cleverly acting as though it were an earlier version of Windows.

Set the Compatibility

(1) Open the Start menu, right-click the program you want to run, and choose Properties from the shortcut menu.

(3) Specify the version of Windows the program was designed for.

(4) Select the check boxes for applying the appropriate restrictions to the display, based on the program's documentation and updated notes from the manufacturer.

> **TIP:** If changing the compatibility mode or the display settings doesn't fix the problem, check with the manufacturer for updated drivers or other fixes.

(2) Select this check box to run the program in compatibility mode.

(5) Click OK. Try running the program. If it still doesn't run, open the Properties dialog box again and change the settings. Continue experimenting until you get the program to work.

> **CAUTION:** Windows XP will remember the compatibility settings between uses for programs that are installed on the computer's hard disk, but it won't remember the compatibility settings for programs that you run from a CD.

> **TIP:** To learn more about compatibility modes, or to run the Program Compatibility Wizard, which can help you identify the settings you need, click the Program Compatibility link in the Properties dialog box.

Starting a Program When Windows Starts

If you always start your workday using the same program, you can have that program start when Windows XP starts. And if you use the same document each day, you can have that document start automatically in the program. Windows XP might take a little longer to load, but your program will be ready for you right away.

Add a Program to the Startup Submenu

① Point to All Programs on the Start menu, and move through the folders until you locate the program you want.

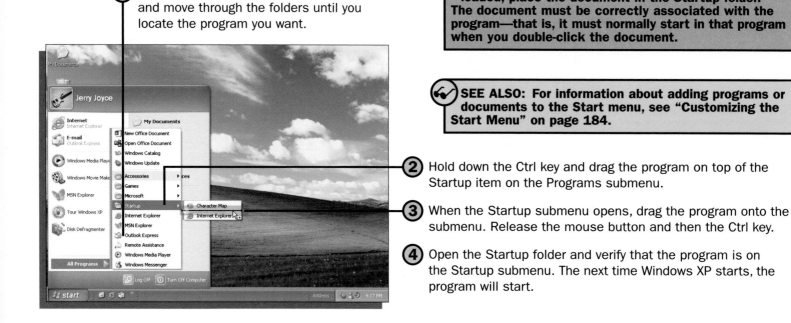

> ⚠ **TIP:** To have a program start with a specific document loaded, place the document in the Startup folder. The document must be correctly associated with the program—that is, it must normally start in that program when you double-click the document.

> ✓ **SEE ALSO:** For information about adding programs or documents to the Start menu, see "Customizing the Start Menu" on page 184.

② Hold down the Ctrl key and drag the program on top of the Startup item on the Programs submenu.

③ When the Startup submenu opens, drag the program onto the submenu. Release the mouse button and then the Ctrl key.

④ Open the Startup folder and verify that the program is on the Startup submenu. The next time Windows XP starts, the program will start.

Changing the Way a Program Starts

Many programs have special *command switches* that you can use to start the program or to modify the way it starts or runs. You can add these commands to the shortcut that starts the program, as well as specify the size of the window and even specify a keyboard shortcut that quickly switches to the program.

Modify the Shortcut

① Locate the shortcut to the program (on the Start menu, on the Desktop, or in a folder). If there is no shortcut to the program or if you're not permitted to modify the existing shortcut, create a new one. Right-click the shortcut, and choose Properties from the shortcut menu.

TRY THIS: Click the Start button, point to All Programs, right-click Outlook Express on the menu that appears, and choose Properties from the shortcut menu. In the Target box on the Shortcut tab, type the command switch /newsonly after the closing quotation marks, and click OK. Open the Start menu, point to All Programs, and choose Outlook Express to open Outlook Express as a news reader only. This is a useful way to connect to newsgroups if you use a program other than Outlook Express—Microsoft Outlook, for example—for your e-mail.

SEE ALSO: For information about creating a shortcut, see "Creating Quick Access to a File or Folder" on page 137.

② Click the Shortcut tab.

③ Add any special command switches, as specified in the program's documentation.

④ If you want to use a keyboard shortcut that switches to the running program, click in the box and press the key combination.

⑤ Specify whether you want to run the program in a normal, a maximized, or a minimized window.

⑥ Modify the comment to change the text shown in the pop-up description when you point to the shortcut.

⑦ Click OK.

Quitting When You're Stuck

If a program isn't working properly and doesn't respond when you try to close it, Windows XP isolates the program so that it doesn't affect your other programs. Provided you're sure that the program really isn't working—as opposed to just taking a long time to do something—you can "end the task." When you use this option, you'll probably lose any unsaved work in the misbehaving program, and, if the problem persists, you might need to reinstall the program.

End the Task

1 When you're sure that the program has stopped working, click the Close button on the program's title bar. You might need to try this several times before you can get the program to respond to your click. Be patient!

My Program (Not Responding)

My Program

You chose to end the nonresponsive program, My Program.

The program is not responding.

Please tell Microsoft about this problem.
We have created an error report that you can send to us. We will treat this report as confidential and anonymous.

To see what data this error report contains, click here.

[Send Error Report] [Don't Send]

TIP: If you can't end a specific program, press Ctrl+Alt+Delete to display the Task Manager. On the Applications tab of the Task Manager dialog box, click the offending program, and then click End Task. If that doesn't work, close all your other running programs, and choose Turn Off from the Shut Down menu in the Task Manager dialog box. If Windows XP is really misbehaving and still doesn't respond, your last resort is to turn off your computer.

SEE ALSO: For information about fixing configuration problems when you restart your computer, see "Starting Up When There's a Problem" on page 222.

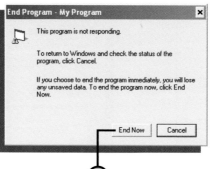

End Program - My Program

This program is not responding.

To return to Windows and check the status of the program, click Cancel.

If you choose to end the program immediately, you will lose any unsaved data. To end the program now, click End Now.

[End Now] [Cancel]

2 If you see a dialog box telling you the program isn't responding, click End Now.

3 When a message appears, click Send Error Report to send technical data about the error over the Internet to Microsoft, or click Don't Send if you want to keep the problem to yourself.

4

Exploring the Internet

Whether you call it the Internet, the Net, or the Web, and whether you use it for business, homework, research, communicating, or shopping, the Web is probably already your window on the world. With that insight in mind, one of the goals of Microsoft Windows XP's designers was to enable you to move between the Web and your own computer in an almost effortless fashion.

If you know the address of the Web page or site you want, you can simply type the address in the Address Bar, and Microsoft Internet Explorer will find and display the page for you. If you don't know the address, you can use the Search feature to search the Internet to find the requested information. Once you've found the page, you can use the *hyperlinks* that you'll find on most pages to navigate from one page or site to another to obtain any additional information you need.

When you start Internet Explorer, it takes you to your *home page,* which is usually a page you've customized to display information that you want to see every day. However, if you want to designate another page as your home page or change some items on the existing home page, you can do so with a couple of mouse-clicks. If there's a page you want to revisit, you can add it to your Favorites list, and Internet Explorer will create a shortcut to that page for you. You can save a Web page and then send it, with all its formatting intact, to friends or colleagues. You can economize on connection charges by saving Web pages and viewing them off line, and you can even set up your computer so that those pages will be updated automatically whenever any of their content changes.

Finding a Web Page

You do most of your navigation on the Internet using the hyperlinks (also called *links* or *jumps*) that are located on Web pages. When you click a link, an Internet address is sent to your Web browser, which looks for the Web site and then displays the requested page. After you've located a Web page, you can explore further if you want. It's a bit like looking up a word in a dictionary and then looking up another word to expand your understanding of the first one.

Explore

Forward button   Stop button

Back button   Search button

Address Bar

If you get lost, click the Home button to return to your home page.

Use a link to jump to another page.

TIP: If you start Internet Explorer from the Start menu, from your Desktop, or from the Quick Launch toolbar, Internet Explorer goes to the page you've designated as your home page. If you start Internet Explorer by clicking a link, choosing a menu command, or using an Internet address, Internet Explorer goes to that specific page and bypasses your home page.

SEE ALSO: For information about changing your home page, see "Setting Your Home Page" on the facing page.

For information about controlling and safeguarding your Internet connection, see "Protecting Personal Information on the Internet" on page 203 and "Restricting Internet Access" on page 204.

(1) Start Internet Explorer if it isn't already running. If you're using a dial-up connection and you aren't already connected to the Internet, connect to your Internet Service Provider (ISP).

(2) From your current page, do any of the following:

- Click the Search button, and search for businesses or individuals or for Web pages that contain specific text.

- Click a relevant link on the page to go to a new page or site.

- Click the Forward or Back button to return to a previously visited site.

- Open the Address Bar drop-down list to specify and jump to a previously visited site, or type a new address to go to that site.

- Click the Stop button to stop downloading a site, and then jump to a different location.

Setting Your Home Page

When you start Internet Explorer, you automatically go to your home page—a page that you might have customized or that contains the links and services you want. If you'd rather use a different home page, or if you want to reset the home page after a service or a program has changed it, you can designate a new home page with just a couple of mouse-clicks.

> **TIP:** If a service provider or an installed program has made substantial changes to the way Internet Explorer looks and works, click the **Restore Defaults** button on the **Advanced** tab of the Internet Options dialog box to return Internet Explorer to its normal functionality.

Reset the Home Page

1 Use Internet Explorer to go to the page you want to use as your home page.

2 Choose Internet Options from the Tools menu.

3 Click Use Current.

4 Click OK.

> **TIP:** If you don't want anyone who uses your computer to review the Internet sites you've visited recently, click the **Clear History** button on the General tab of the Internet Options dialog box.

> **CAUTION:** Some service providers don't allow you to change your home page. You're required to use the service's home page until you're properly logged on. If this is the case, your only recourse is to complain loudly to that service provider.

Returning to Your Favorite Sites

When you find a good source of information or entertainment, you don't need to waste a lot of time searching for that site the next time you want to visit it. You can simply add the site to your Favorites list, and Internet Explorer will obligingly create a shortcut to the site for you.

> **TIP:** If you want to return to a Web page but you didn't save it in your Favorites list, click the History button and search for the page by the time period in which you visited it.

Save a Location

(1) Go to the site whose location you want to save.

(2) Choose Add To Favorites from the Favorites menu to display the Add Favorite dialog box.

(4) Click OK.

(3) Type a name for the site, or use the proposed name.

> **TIP:** If you'll be storing many different favorite locations, click the Create In button in the Add Favorite dialog box and create a file structure for your pages.

Return to a Location

(1) Click Favorites on the Standard Buttons toolbar.

(2) In the Favorites Explorer Bar, click the name of the site you want to return to. If the site is contained in a subfolder, click the folder and then click the site.

Saving a Web Page

If a Web page contains important information that you know you'll want to refer to in the future, you can save the page on your computer. The way you save it, however, affects which information will be available when you open the saved page. After you've saved the Web page, you can send it to friends and colleagues if you want.

Save a Web Page

(1) Start Internet Explorer if it isn't already running, and connect to the Internet if you aren't already connected. Go to the Web page you want to save.

(2) Choose Save As from the File menu to display the Save Web Page dialog box.

TIP: If you're planning to send a Web page to someone, save the page as a Web Archive so that the single file will contain all the elements of the Web page. The recipient will need to have Internet Explorer version 4 or later (or a similar browser) installed on his or her computer to be able to read a Web Archive file.

CAUTION: Sometimes, although certain items on a Web page appear to be text, they're actually graphics elements. This is usually the case when the designer of the page or site wanted to include some special formatting that couldn't be done with normal HTML formatting. If you save the page either as Web Page, HTML Only or as Text File, the information that has that type of special formatting won't be saved.

(4) Type a name for the file, or use the proposed name.

(5) Click in the list to specify the way you want the Web page to be saved:

- Web Page Complete to save the formatted text and layout and to place all the linked resources, such as pictures, in a separate folder

- Web Archive, Single File to create a single archive file that contains all the elements of the Web page

- Web Page, HTML Only to save the formatted text and layout but none of the linked items, such as pictures

- Text File to save only the text

(3) If you don't want to save the document to the default folder, specify a different location, drive, or folder.

(6) Click Save.

Viewing Web Pages Off Line

If you aren't always connected to the Internet, or if you simply want to economize on connection charges, you can store the Web pages you want and then read them off line at your leisure. And if there are Web sites that you visit frequently, you can set up your computer so that the stored Web pages will be updated, or *synchronized,* automatically when the information in them changes. That way, you'll always have the most recent version of the Web page.

Store a Web Page

1 Start Internet Explorer if it isn't already running, and connect to the Internet if you aren't already connected. Go to the Web page you want to store.

2 Choose Add To Favorites from the Favorites menu to display the Add Favorite dialog box.

3 Select this check box to store the Web page.

4 Click Customize.

> **SEE ALSO: For information about deleting all your offline files from your hard disk, see "Maintaining Your Computer" on page 215.**

5 Step through the Offline Favorite Wizard, specifying whether

- Pages linked to this page are also to be stored.

- Web pages are to be updated manually or automatically, and, if automatically, specifying the schedule for updating.

- A password is required, and, if so, specifying your user name and password.

6 Click Finish, and wait for the Web page or pages to be synchronized.

7 Repeat steps 2 through 6 for any other pages you want to view off line. Disconnect from Internet Explorer when you've finished.

View an Offline Web Page

① With your computer *not* connected to the Internet, start Internet Explorer if it isn't already running. If the computer keeps trying to connect, choose Work Offline from the File menu.

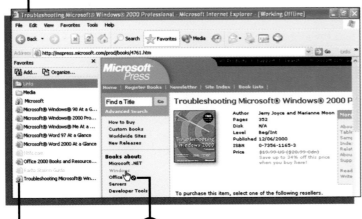

③ Read the page. Note that the mouse pointer indicates when you can't use a link in the offline page.

② Open the Favorites menu or the Favorites Explorer pane, and click the Web page in the list. Note that files set for offline viewing display a different icon than do files available only while you're on line.

> ✋ **CAUTION: Offline Web pages use a large amount of disk space, especially if you choose to save pages that are linked to your main page. If your disk space is limited, be selective about the Web pages you store.**

> ❗ **TIP: Even if you've set up your offline Web pages to be synchronized automatically, use the Synchronize command when you want to update a page manually.**

Synchronize Your Offline Web Pages

① Connect to the Internet if you aren't already connected.

② Choose Synchronize from Internet Explorer's Tools menu or from the Accessories submenu of the Start menu to display the Items To Synchronize dialog box.

④ Click Synchronize.

③ Select the check boxes (if they aren't already selected) for the Web pages you want to be automatically updated, and clear the check boxes for the Web pages you don't want to be updated.

⑤ Wait for the pages to be synchronized.

Copying Material from a Web Page

Sometimes, although you might want to save one or two items from a Web page, you have no use for the entire page. It's a simple matter to save only the parts of the page you want.

CAUTION: When you copy material from a Web page, make sure that you're not violating any copyrights.

Save a Picture

1 Right-click the picture, and choose Save Picture As from the shortcut menu.

2 If you don't want to save the picture to the default My Pictures folder, specify a different location, drive, or folder.

3 Type a name for the file, or use the proposed name.

4 Specify the format you want for the picture.

5 Click Save.

Save Some Text

1 Click at the beginning of the text you want to copy. You won't see an insertion point, but Internet Explorer is smart—it knows where you clicked.

3 Choose Copy from the Edit menu.

2 Drag the mouse over the text you want to copy.

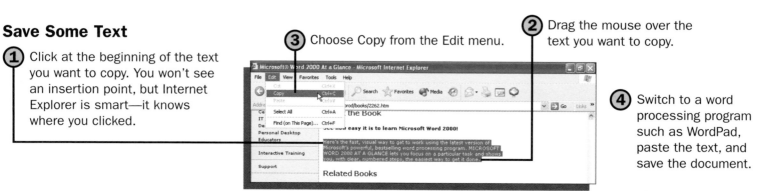

4 Switch to a word processing program such as WordPad, paste the text, and save the document.

Finding Something on the Internet

To search for a specific item on the Internet—a list of sources where you can buy other *Plain & Simple* books, for example, or the menu and locator map for that new restaurant you want to try—you can jump right to a search page and set up your query. Once the results are displayed, you can jump to the page that contains the information you're looking for, and, if it's not what you want, you can try another page.

> ! **TIP:** You can search from any folder window or from Internet Explorer by clicking the Search button on the Standard Buttons toolbar.

Search for an Item

(1) Click the Start button, and choose Search from the Start menu to display the Search Results dialog box. Connect to the Internet if you aren't already connected.

(2) Click Search The Internet.

(3) Click a category. Click More to see additional categories.

(4) Type the information you want. Drag the border between the Search Explorer Bar and the main window if you need more room.

(5) Click Search.

(6) Click a link, and view the item you want.

(8) Close the Search Explorer Bar when you've finished with the search results.

(7) To see other results, click a relevant link, and view the item.

Exploring with MSN Explorer

MSN (The Microsoft Network) Explorer is a customized Web browser that contains connections to various MSN Web sites. MSN Explorer also provides a helpful environment for reading and sending e-mail using either a Hotmail account or an MSN e-mail account.

Explore

(1) Click the Start button, and choose MSN Explorer from the Start menu. If you're using MSN Explorer for the first time, go through the sign-up process.

(3) Use the links to connect to your personal content.

(4) Click to customize your personal settings.

(5) Click to listen to music, radio broadcasts, or other content using Windows Media Player.

CAUTION: If you have an MSN e-mail account but you start using MSN Explorer for reading and sending your mail, your MSN e-mail account will be converted from a POP3 format to an HTTP format. This can be a problem if you sometimes use a mail program other than MSN Explorer to read your mail and that program doesn't support the HTTP mail format. In that case, you won't be able to use that program to read the e-mail from your MSN e-mail account, and you'll need to use MSN Explorer, or another program such as Outlook Express, to read the HTTP format.

(2) Use the links to go to specific sites, to read and compose mail, and to connect to chats, Web communities, or instant messaging. Most of the links provided by MSN Explorer will take you to Web sites that are part of MSN.

(6) Click Help & Settings to change your password, customize your home page and MSN Explorer, or change settings for your mail.

(7) Type a Web address in the Address Bar, click a location in your Favorites list, or use links to go to any page on the Web.

5 Communicating

The ability to communicate electronically is one of a computer's most used and most valued features. In this section, we'll discuss the tools that Microsoft Windows XP provides to enable you to reach out and connect with other people.

Microsoft Outlook Express helps you organize and customize your e-mail and does double duty as a news reader. It can complete an address from your Contacts list when you type only the first couple of letters of your contact's name, and it can automatically add a signature to your messages. You can format your e-mail messages with fonts and colors, and you can choose or create your own e-mail stationery. If you often send one message to the same group of people, you can combine all their addresses into a *group* so that you don't have to enter each individual's address. You can enclose files, or *attachments,* with your e-mail, and if an attached file exceeds the size that your mail system can handle, you can *compress* the file to make it smaller.

You can use Windows Messenger to exchange instant text messages or to conduct working sessions with as many as five of your contacts whenever they're on line. If text conversations aren't personal enough, you can even have voice and video chats with your contacts, provided they're running Windows XP. In a Windows Messenger session, you can share programs or discuss documents on line, you can use the Whiteboard to add notes or drawings to emphasize a point or raise a question, and you can transfer large files without compressing them.

Sending E-Mail

You don't have to address an envelope or trek to the mailbox on a cold, rainy day. All you do is select a name, create a message, and click a Send button. Outlook Express and your mail server do the rest. What could be more convenient?

Create a Message

(1) Open Outlook Express from the Start menu. Click Create Mail. If you want to send a formatted message with a background and coordinated fonts and bullets, click the down arrow next to the button, and click the stationery you want to use.

(6) Click Send to send the message to your Outbox.

(4) Press the Tab key to move to the Subject line, type a subject, and press Tab again to move into the message area.

(2) Start typing the recipient's name. Press Enter when Outlook Express completes the name based on the names in your Contacts list, or continue typing if the proposed name is incorrect. To add more names, type a semicolon (;), and then start typing another recipient's name.

(3) Press the Tab key to move to the CC field, and type the names of the people who are to receive a copy of the message.

(7) When you've composed all the messages you want to send, click Send/Recv to send the messages in the Outbox to your mail server.

Formatting tools

(5) Type your message. Use any of the formatting tools to format your message.

SEE ALSO: For information about adding formatting, pictures, or your signature, see "Designing Your Default Message" on page 56.

For information about setting up e-mail accounts in Outlook Express, see "Setting Up Outlook Express" on page 170.

CAUTION: A formatted message uses HTML formatting. Use Plain Text formatting if you're not sure whether the recipient has a mail reader that supports HTML formatting. Messages using Plain Text formatting are smaller and will download faster over a slow Internet connection than will messages using HTML formatting, especially those that contain pictures.

Receiving and Reading E-Mail

Outlook Express lets you specify how frequently you want it to check for incoming e-mail, and it notifies you when you receive new mail. You can check your Inbox and see at a glance which messages have and haven't been read, or you can set the view to list unread messages only.

Read Your Messages

(2) On the View menu, specify how you want to view your messages:

- Point to Current View, and choose the type of messages you want displayed.
- Point to Sort By, and choose the way you want the messages to be ordered.
- Choose Layout, specify whether and where you want the preview pane displayed, and click OK.

(1) Switch to the Inbox for the mail service you want to view if it isn't the currently active folder.

(3) Click a message header, and read the message in the preview pane.

TIP: When you start Outlook Express, it checks for your mail, and it checks periodically thereafter while it's running. To receive mail immediately when you don't want to wait for the system to check your mailbox for you, click the Send/Recv button. To change the frequency with which Outlook Express checks for mail, choose Options from the Tools menu, and change the settings on the General tab.

(4) Double-click a message header to view the message in a separate window.

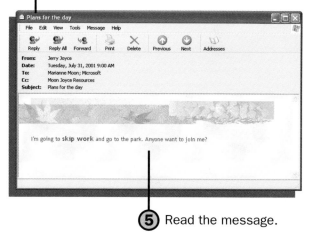

(5) Read the message.

TRY THIS: On the Read tab of the Options dialog box, click the Fonts button. Click a different font in the Proportional Font list and a different font size in the Font Size list, and click OK. Close the Options dialog box, and look at the messages in the preview pane.

Designing Your Default Message

Why not let your computer do some of your work for you? When you design a default mail message, every new message that you start will look exactly the way you want, with all the elements in place—a specific background picture, your signature automatically inserted at the end of the message, a font that makes the message a little more "you," and so on.

Add a Signature

1 In Outlook Express, choose Options from the Tools menu, and click the Signatures tab of the Options dialog box.

2 Click New.

3 Type the signature you want to use as your default signature, or specify the text or HTML document that contains the signature.

5 If you have more than one mail or news account, click Advanced.

6 Select the check boxes for the accounts that will use this signature, and then click OK.

4 Specify whether you want the signature added automatically to all outgoing messages and whether or not you want it included in replies and forwarded messages.

> **TIP:** If you know that a certain contact can receive only plain-text–formatted messages, right-click his or her name in your Contacts list, choose Properties from the shortcut menu, and, on the Name tab, select the Send E-Mail Using Plain Text check box. Click OK. To send a message in plain text only once, choose Plain Text from the Format menu when you compose the message.

> **TIP:** If your message is in the HTML format, your signature file can be an HTML document too. If you enjoy experimenting with HTML, you can create anything from an attractive or ornate signature to a humorous or truly obnoxious one. The signature file, however, can't be any larger than 4 KB.

Specify Your Stationery

1 Click the Compose tab of the Options dialog box, and turn on this check box to use stationery.

3 In the list, click the stationery you want to use.

2 Click Select.

4 Click OK.

5 Click Apply.

6 Click the Send tab, and click the HTML option for your mail format if it isn't already selected.

7 Click OK.

> **!** **TIP:** To create your own e-mail stationery, click the Create New button on the Compose tab of the Options dialog box, and complete the Stationery Setup Wizard.

> **✋** **CAUTION:** Although you can use stationery and other formatting in a news message, many newsgroups either require or suggest that you use plain-text formatting to keep your messages to a manageable size.

Sending or Receiving a File

A great way to share a file—a Microsoft Word document, a picture, or even an entire program—is to include it as part of an e-mail message. The file is kept as a separate part of the message—an *attachment*—that the recipient can save and open at any time.

Send a File by E-Mail

③ Click OK.

TIP: Some mail systems can't accommodate attachments larger than about 1 MB, and some types of files can be corrupted when they're sent as attachments. In those cases, you can compress the file before you send it. To do so, send the file to a compressed folder, and then e-mail the compressed folder. You can also use other file-transfer methods such as those available through FTP services or Windows Messenger.

SEE ALSO: For information about other ways to transfer files, see "Transferring Files" on page 66.

For information about using compressed folders, see "Compressing Files" on page 132.

① Open the folder window that contains the file, right-click the file, point to Send To on the shortcut menu, and choose Mail Recipient from the submenu.

② If you receive a message about modifying the file you're sending, click the option you want.

⑤ Click Send to send the message just as you'd send any other message.

④ Address the message, and type your message text.

Receive an Attachment

(1) Select a message you've received that contains an attachment.

(2) Click the Attachment icon, and, from the menu that appears, choose

- The name of the file to open the file.

- Save Attachments to save the file to disk without opening it.

(3) If you chose to save the file, select it.

(5) Click Save.

(4) Specify where you want to save the file.

> **CAUTION:** Viruses are often distributed in attached files. *Never* open an attachment you aren't expecting without first saving the attachment to disk and then using a virus-scanning program to inspect the file.

> **TRY THIS:** Open a folder window, and select two or more files. Right-click one of the files, point to Send To on the shortcut menu, and choose Mail Recipient from the submenu. In your message, click the Attach button, and use the Insert Attachment dialog box to locate an additional file in a different folder. Select the file, and click Attach. You now have multiple files enclosed in a single message.

Replying to or Forwarding a Message

When you receive an e-mail message that needs a reply or that you want to forward to someone else, all it takes is a click of a button to create a new message. But be careful when you use the Reply All button—your message could be received by a lot of people for whom it wasn't intended!

> ⚠ **TIP:** When you reply to a message that has an attached file, the attachment isn't included with your reply. When you forward a message, though, the attachment is included so that the recipient can open or save it.

Reply to or Forward a Message

① Select the message header.

② Click the appropriate button:
- Reply to send your reply to the writer of the message only
- Reply All to send your reply to the writer of the message and to everyone listed in the original message's To and CC lines
- Forward to send a copy of the message to another recipient

③ Add names to or delete names from the To and CC lines.

The original header information and message text are included.

⑤ Click Send.

④ Type your reply message or any note associated with the forwarded message.

Subscribing to Newsgroups

With so many newsgroups available, you'll probably want to be selective about the ones you review. You can do so in Outlook Express by *subscribing* to the newsgroups you like. Those newsgroups will appear in the message pane when you select the news server and will also appear on the Folders Bar, if it's displayed, when you expand the listing for a news server.

Specify Your Newsgroups

(1) With Outlook Express open and connected to the Internet, click the news server you want to access.

(3) If no dialog box appears, click Newsgroups.

TIP: To see the full names of the newsgroups, drag the boundary between the Newsgroup and Description labels to widen the Newsgroup area.

SEE ALSO: For information about setting up your news servers, see "Setting Up Outlook Express" on page 170.

(2) If you receive a notification that you're not subscribed to any newsgroups, click Yes.

(4) If you have more than one news server, specify the one you want to use.

(5) Type a keyword to search for the newsgroups you want to access.

(7) Click OK.

(6) Double-click a newsgroup to subscribe to it. Repeat to subscribe to all the newsgroups you want to access.

Reading and Writing the News

Reading and adding to the news—or the gossip, tirades, and misinformation that often pass for news in Internet newsgroups—is as simple as reading or sending your e-mail. All you need to do is specify a newsgroup and select a message, and then either read the message or click a button to respond to it.

> **! TIP:** A "thread" is a series of messages in which one person posts a message and other readers reply to the message and/or to the replies.

Select a Message

> **! TIP:** To open the news message in a separate window, double-click the message.

(2) On the View menu, point to Current View, and choose the view you want:

- Show All Messages to see everything
- Hide Read Messages to display only the messages you haven't read
- Show Downloaded Messages to see the messages you've downloaded
- Hide Read Or Ignored Messages to display only the messages you haven't read or that haven't been marked to be ignored
- Show Replies To My Messages to see responses to your messages

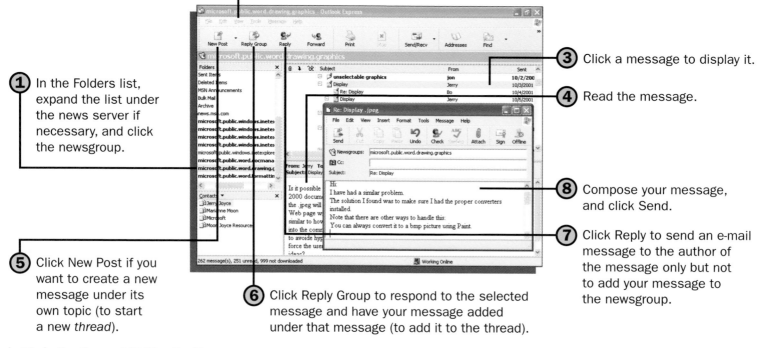

(1) In the Folders list, expand the list under the news server if necessary, and click the newsgroup.

(3) Click a message to display it.

(4) Read the message.

(8) Compose your message, and click Send.

(7) Click Reply to send an e-mail message to the author of the message only but not to add your message to the newsgroup.

(5) Click New Post if you want to create a new message under its own topic (to start a new *thread*).

(6) Click Reply Group to respond to the selected message and have your message added under that message (to add it to the thread).

Reading E-Mail and News Off Line

If you aren't always connected to the mail and news servers, or if you want to economize on connection charges, you can download your e-mail and newsgroup messages, disconnect from the Internet, and then read the messages at your leisure. Any replies or new messages you compose will be stored in your Outbox until you reconnect.

Download the Messages

(1) Click the mail or news service whose content you want to read off line.

(2) Click Settings, and specify what you want to be downloaded.

(5) Wait for the messages to download, and then disconnect from the Internet.

(6) Click a message to read it. If Outlook Express tries to reconnect, choose Work Offline from the File menu, and then click the message to read it.

(3) Select the check boxes for the folders or groups you want to download. Clear the check boxes for those you don't want to download.

(4) Click Synchronize Account. Connect to the Internet if you aren't already connected.

> **! TIP: Unless you've changed some settings, all your messages are automatically downloaded from a POP3 e-mail service. However, messages aren't routinely downloaded from an HTTP service (a Hotmail account, for example) or an IMAP service. Use the method described in the procedure on this page to download any messages from those mail services that you want to review off line.**

Managing Your E-Mail Contacts

When you're using e-mail, you don't need to type an address every time you send a message; you can retrieve addresses from your Contacts list. All the names shown in the Contacts list are actually stored in your Address Book, a separate program that works with Outlook Express and other programs. If you frequently send one message to the same group of people, you can gather all their addresses into a *group,* and then all you need to find and use is that one address item. It's a real time-saver.

Create a New Contact

1 In Outlook Express, point to New on the File menu, and choose Contact from the submenu to display the Properties dialog box.

2 On the various tabs of the Properties dialog box, enter the information you want to record.

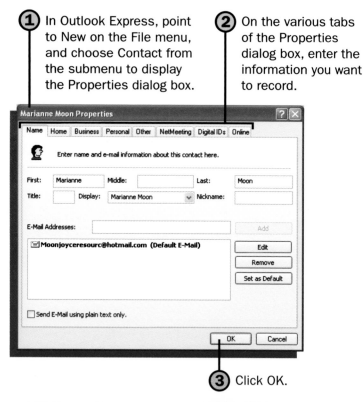

3 Click OK.

> **!** **TIP: To automatically add to your Address Book the addresses of all the people whose messages you reply to, choose Options from the Tools menu, and, on the Send tab, select the Automatically Put People I Reply To In My Address Book check box.**

Add an Address from a Message

1 In the Inbox, right-click the message.

2 Choose Add Sender To Address Book from the shortcut menu. If the command is grayed (unavailable), connect to the Internet or to your mail server, click the message to download it, and then right-click it and choose the command again.

> **!** **TIP: To add to your Address Book someone whose name is listed in the CC line of a message, double-click the message to open it in a separate window, and then right-click the name you want to add.**

Create a Group

① Click Addresses on the toolbar.

② On the Address Book toolbar, click New, and choose New Group from the menu.

③ On the Group tab of the Properties dialog box, type a descriptive name, or *alias,* for the group.

④ Click Select Members.

⑤ Click the name of someone you want to include in the group.

⑥ Click Select. Continue selecting members and clicking the Select button until the Members list is complete.

⑧ Click OK.

⑨ Add any further information to the Group Details tab, and click OK. Close the Address Book when you've finished.

⑦ Use the New Contact button or the Name and Members boxes to add to the group any new members who aren't listed in your Address Book.

TIP: You can collect addresses from address books from other computers, other programs, or other users by using the Import command on the File menu, by clicking the Find button on the address book's toolbar to use a directory service, or by opening and importing an electronic business card *(vCard)* that someone sent you. (A vCard, or virtual card, is a file that contains a single Address Book entry with contact information for an individual.)

Transferring Files

In most cases, transferring files is a simple task: if you want to transfer a few small files, you can easily send them by e-mail or copy them to a removable disk. On a network, you can simply move the files to a shared folder. If you're not connected to a business network, you can connect using a dial-up server or a VPN (Virtual Private Network) connection over the Internet. However, if you need to transfer a number of large files but you don't have access to a network, there are several possible solutions. Listed below are additional methods for directly transferring files; you should find at least one among them that's appropriate for your situation. To find more information about any of these methods, look in the index of this book and/or search the Windows XP Help And Support Center.

Direct Network Connection: A direct network connection connects two computers with a special cable, using either the serial or parallel port on each computer or an infrared link. Once the computers are connected, you've established a network connection through which you have access to shared folders and files. However, this method works only with Windows-based computers.

HyperTerminal: HyperTerminal is a communications program that enables you to call and connect to another computer over a telephone line. The other computer must have a communications package (either HyperTerminal or a compatible program). You can select from a list of different standard transfer protocols. You can use HyperTerminal to connect to different types of computers and operating systems and to access Telnet computer services.

Windows Messenger: Send a file to or receive a file from any online contact. The recipient must agree to receive the file before you can send it.

Dial-Up Server: You can set up your own computer as a dial-up server so that other computers can call in to connect and establish a network link through which files can be transferred to and from the server.

FTP Transfer: You can use FTP (File Transfer Protocol) to transfer files to an FTP server over the Internet. In most cases you'll be able to use Internet Explorer to connect and manage files.

Windows XP also provides two invaluable tools to assist you in transferring files: the Compressed Folders feature and the Windows Briefcase.

Compressed Folders: The Compressed Folders feature reduces the size of the files it contains and keeps all the compressed files in one location. When you transfer a compressed folder, the receiving computer sees either a compressed folder (if the Compressed Folders feature is installed) or a ZIP-type file that can be opened using one of several third-party programs.

Windows Briefcase: The Windows Briefcase is a file-management tool. It helps you keep track of different versions of a file when the file has been edited on different computers. You copy files from your computer to the Briefcase and transfer the entire Briefcase to another computer, where the files can be edited and saved back into the Briefcase. When you return the Briefcase to your computer, the original files on your computer can be updated automatically.

Adding Online Contacts

Using Windows Messenger and a *Passport,* you can exchange instant messages with your designated contacts whenever they're on line. For you to be able to contact others, they must be in your Contacts list. You can add a person who has a Passport to your list, or you can send e-mail to someone who doesn't have a Passport to provide that person with information about obtaining a Passport and using the proper Windows Messenger software.

Add a Contact

① Connect to the Internet if you aren't already connected.

② Double-click the Windows Messenger icon in the notification area of the taskbar. If you don't see the icon, click the Start button, point to All Programs, and choose Windows Messenger from the submenu to open the Windows Messenger dialog box.

TIP: In most cases, when you set up Windows XP, you also set up your e-mail account and your Passport. If you didn't, however, or if you want to change your Passport, choose Control Panel from the Start menu, click User Accounts, and then click your user name.

TRY THIS: In Outlook Express, click the down arrow next to Contacts, choose New Online Contact from the menu, and add a new contact. Click an existing e-mail contact, open the Contacts menu again, and choose Set As Online Contact. Point to a contact's name and see whether that person is on line. If so, right-click the contact's name, and then choose Send Instant Message from the shortcut menu.

③ After you've logged on, click Add.

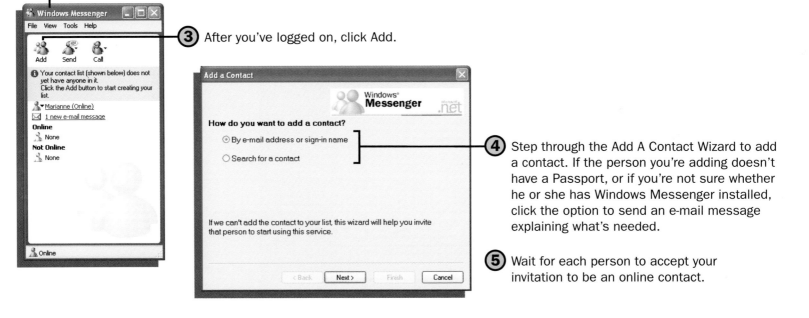

④ Step through the Add A Contact Wizard to add a contact. If the person you're adding doesn't have a Passport, or if you're not sure whether he or she has Windows Messenger installed, click the option to send an e-mail message explaining what's needed.

⑤ Wait for each person to accept your invitation to be an online contact.

Sending Instant Messages

Are you and your contacts ready for an online conversation? Each of your contacts must have a Passport and must have the Windows Messenger software installed. You can have as many as 75 different contacts and can include up to 5 people in a text conversation. Each message can contain up to 400 characters.

Have a Conversation On Line

1 Connect to the Internet if you aren't already connected.

2 Click the Windows Messenger icon in the notification area of the taskbar. On the menu that appears, point to Send An Instant Message, and choose the person you want to connect to.

7 Click the Windows Messenger icon in the notification area, point to My Status on the menu, and choose the status you want.

3 Read the message from the other person.

4 Type your text message, and press Enter to send it.

> **!** **TIP:** Instant messaging procedures and protocols change frequently. You'll probably need to upgrade the software periodically to maintain complete functionality.

> **!** **TIP:** You can play a game over the Internet with one of your contacts. Each of you must have the game installed on your computer, and the game must be designed for Internet play. To start a game, click the Invite button and invite your contact to play.

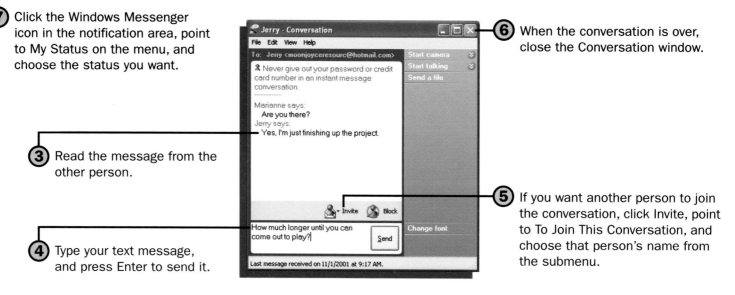

6 When the conversation is over, close the Conversation window.

5 If you want another person to join the conversation, click Invite, point to To Join This Conversation, and choose that person's name from the submenu.

Having a Voice and Video Chat ⊕ NEW FEATURE

If a text conversation is too antiquated or too impersonal for your taste, you can use both voice and video in your instant messages. If you and your contact are both using Windows Messenger on computers running Windows XP, and you both have the necessary sound systems and video cameras, having a voice and video chat is as simple as clicking a button.

Have a Chat

 1 Connect to the Internet if you aren't already connected.

2 Click the Windows Messenger icon in the notification area of the taskbar. On the menu that appears, point to Send An Instant Message, and choose the person with whom you want to chat to open the Conversation dialog box.

> **!** **TIP: The first time you ran Windows Messenger, you should have stepped through the Audio And Tuning Wizard. If you find that your sound system needs some adjustment, close your conversation, double-click the Windows Messenger icon in the notification area of the taskbar, and, in the Windows Messenger window, choose Audio And Tuning Wizard from the Tools menu to retune your system.**

3 Do either of the following:

- To have a video and voice conversation, click Start Camera, and wait for the other person to accept the invitation.
- To have a voice-only conversation, click Start Talking, and wait for the other person to accept the invitation.

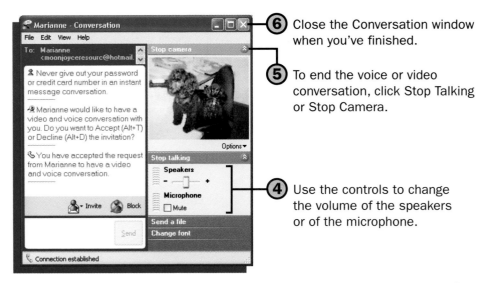

6 Close the Conversation window when you've finished.

5 To end the voice or video conversation, click Stop Talking or Stop Camera.

4 Use the controls to change the volume of the speakers or of the microphone.

Sharing Items with Your Contacts ⊕ NEW FEATURE

If you need to display a program to one of your contacts, or if you want to allow the other person to use the program or to gain access to a folder on your computer, all you need to do is start a conversation, and then you can share the program or folder.

Share a Program or a Folder

1 On your computer, open the program, folder, or document you want to share.

2 Start a Windows Messenger conversation with the person with whom you want to share the item. Invite others into the conversation if you want.

3 Click Invite, and choose To Start Application Sharing. Wait for the other person to accept the invitation. (If you're connected to more than one contact, you'll need to click Invite, point to To Start Application Sharing, and click the name of the contact you want to invite.)

CAUTION: If you share the Desktop and then allow the other person to control the Desktop or your shared programs, he or she will have full control of your computer and will be able to access anything from the Start menu. Even if you share only one program, the other person can make considerable modifications to your settings and files. Never leave your computer unattended when you're sharing items and you've given someone else control.

4 Select the item that's going to be shared.

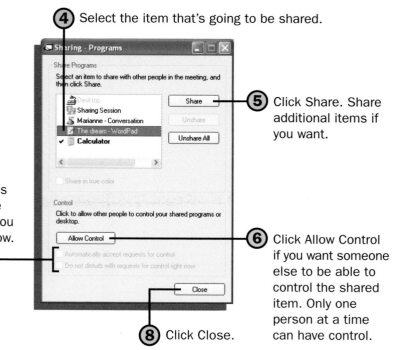

5 Click Share. Share additional items if you want.

7 Select the check boxes for the type of control you want to allow.

6 Click Allow Control if you want someone else to be able to control the shared item. Only one person at a time can have control.

8 Click Close.

SEE ALSO: For information about asking someone for help using remote assistance, see "Helping Each Other" on page 226.

Use the Shared Item

1 Click in the item to be displayed on both computers, and make sure there's nothing on your Desktop that might obscure the other person's view of the item. Make any changes you want.

5 To make changes to what is shared, click App Sharing, and make your changes in the Sharing Programs dialog box.

6 When you've finished, click Close to end the sharing session.

2 If you're allowing control by others, a person who wants to take control should choose Request Control from the Control menu. If a dialog box appears asking whether you want to let that person take control, click Accept or Reject.

4 To regain control, click your mouse.

3 Let the other person make the desired changes.

! **TIP:** Because of the resources that are required, if you're using video or voice conferencing, you can be connected to only one other contact. If you aren't using video or voice conferencing, you can share a program with up to five other people.

! **TIP:** You can share and play certain games using Windows Messenger. To play a game, it must be installed on both computers and configured to be played over Windows Messenger. See the game's documentation for the proper settings.

Illustrating Your Conversation ⊕ NEW FEATURE

It's a nice convenience during a Windows Messenger conversation to have a place where you can jot down a few notes or scribble a quick drawing to illustrate a point. Windows Messenger provides the Whiteboard for exactly that purpose. When you use the Whiteboard during a conversation with an online contact, the notes or drawings that either of you make are visible to both of you.

> **! TIP: Although the Whiteboard looks a lot like another Windows program called Paint, it functions quite differently. Once you've created a note or a drawing on the Whiteboard, you can use the Selector tool to select the item, drag it to a new location, apply different formatting (color, for example), stack one item on top of another, or delete the item.**

Use the Whiteboard

(1) Start a Windows Messenger conversation with the person you want to confer with. Invite others to join the conversation if you want.

(2) Click Invite, and choose To Start Whiteboard. Wait for the other person to accept the invitation. If you're connected to more than one contact, click Invite, point to To Start Whiteboard again, and choose the other contacts you want to invite.

Paste almost anything that you can copy to the Clipboard.

Use text to make a point.

(5) If you want to save the contents of the Whiteboard for later viewing, choose Save from the File menu.

(6) Close the Whiteboard when you've finished.

Position the Remote Pointer to point out an item.

(3) Use the tools to create your illustrations and notes.

(4) To paste an item from a different program onto the Whiteboard, copy the item (press Ctrl+C) to the Windows Clipboard, and then paste the item (press Ctrl+V) onto the Whiteboard.

Add a blank page.

Use the graphics tools to create callouts.

Highlight text, or anything else, for emphasis.

Go to different pages of the Whiteboard.

Sending a File by Windows Messenger

One of the easiest ways to transfer a file from one computer to another over the Internet is to use Windows Messenger, especially if you're sending a large file. When you send a file as an e-mail attachment, you're often limited as to its size (usually it can be no larger than 1 MB), but when you use Windows Messenger there's no limitation on file size.

Send a File

(1) Use Windows Messenger to connect to the person to whom you'll be sending the file.

(3) Locate and select the file to be sent.

(4) Click Open, and wait for the recipient to accept the file.

(2) Choose Send A File from the File menu. If you're connected to more than one person, point to Send A File To on the File menu, and choose the person to whom you want to send the file. (You can send a file to only one person at a time.)

Formatting Your Message

When you use Windows Messenger to communicate with others, you can format your messages with the fonts and colors of your choice. You can also use *emoticons*—those little symbols that some people love and others just can't stand—instead of words.

> ! **TIP:** When you specify a font size, only the size of the text on *your* computer is affected. Text size is controlled by each individual computer.

Format the Text

(1) In your Conversation window, click Change Font to display the Change My Message Font dialog box.

(3) Click OK.

(2) Specify the font, font style, size, effect, and color you want, and then view the result in the Sample box.

(4) Type and send your newly formatted message.

Use Emoticons

(1) Use Windows Messenger to connect to a friend or colleague.

(2) In your message, type the appropriate characters to convey your sentiments.

> ! **TIP:** If you don't see the emoticons, choose Show Emoticons from the Edit menu. For more information about using emoticons, see the Windows Messenger Help file.

6

Working with Pictures and Movies

NEW FEATURE

Drawings and paintings, illustrations in magazines, photographs of people, pets, and places…we all love pictures. Whether you want to enliven your documents with original drawings or add family photographs to your e-mail or your Web page, Microsoft Windows XP provides the tools that will help you achieve professional-looking results.

You can create your own drawings or edit existing ones in the Paint program, using Paint's tools to create the effects you want. Even if you're not a great artist, it can be a lot of fun! However, you're not limited to Paint's *bitmap* images. Windows XP was designed to enable you to work confidently with digital images as well. With help from the Scanner And Camera Wizard, you can easily scan images directly into your computer or into any graphics program that's designed to accept scanned images. With a couple of mouse-clicks, you can also review, select, and download photographs from a digital camera into your computer. You can organize your pictures in the special pictures-friendly My Pictures folder that Windows XP provides, or you can create your own customized folders to house the picture-storage system that works best for you.

Another exciting tool that comes with Windows XP is Windows Movie Maker, which enables you to make great little movies from a variety of sources—you can use a digital video camera, a digital Web camera, existing video clips, material from an analog video camera or from videotape or still pictures. You can edit your clips, create fade-in/fade-out transitions between clips, and add an audio track, a musical soundtrack, background sounds, or a narration.

Drawing a Picture

If you're feeling artistic, you can create a picture in Paint. The Paint program comes with Windows XP and was designed to create and edit bitmap pictures in a variety of formats. Although you can print your picture if you want to, Paint pictures are usually inserted into other documents. You can also create a Paint picture and use it as the wallpaper for your Desktop.

TIP: A bitmap is just that: a map created from small dots, or *bits*. It's a lot like a piece of graph paper with some squares filled in and others left blank to create a picture. Different formats often have different amounts of information about the picture, and they store the information in different ways. The JPEG format, for example, generally reduces the size of a file, whereas a TIF-formatted file contains additional information and can produce a very high-quality picture.

Create a Picture

(1) Start the Paint program from the Accessories submenu of the Start menu.

(2) Choose Attributes from the Image menu to display the Attributes dialog box, and set the dimensions of your drawing.

(3) Click OK.

(4) Click a drawing tool.

(5) Click an option for the selected tool. (Note that options aren't available for all tools.)

(7) Click to start the drawing, and drag the end or the corner of the shape to create the shape you want. Continue experimenting with different tools to complete your picture.

Sample of the foreground color

Sample of the background color

(6) Click the color you want to use. Use the left mouse button to select the foreground color and the right mouse button to select the background color.

Rectangular dimension (in pixels) of the current drawing element

Current location (in pixels) of a tool, or of the starting point of the drawing

TRY THIS: Start a new Paint picture, and set the picture's Width and Height to the dimensions of your screen in pixels (800 x 600, for example). Create and save your picture, and then choose Set As Wallpaper (Centered) from the File menu.

Use the Tools

Polygon tool

Line tool

Text tool

Fill With Color tool

Rectangle tool

Ellipse tool

Rounded Rectangle tool

1 Drag the shapes you want by holding down

● The left mouse button to drag with the foreground color.

● The right mouse button to drag with the background color.

● The Shift key to modify the function of some of the tools, as shown in the table below.

Airbrush tool

Brush tool

Curve tool

Pencil tool

Change a Tool's Function with the Shift Key

Hold down the Shift key and	Result
The Ellipse tool	Creates a circle.
The Rectangle tool	Creates a square.
The Rounded Rectangle tool	Creates a square with rounded corners.
The Line tool	Draws a horizontal, vertical, or diagonal line.

TIP: To add text to a picture, use the Text tool to draw a text box, and just start typing. As long as the text box is active, you can edit the text, change the font, and resize the text box. When you click outside the text box, the text is turned into a bitmap image that can be edited just like any other picture element.

TIP: A bitmap picture can create a very large file, depending on the resolution and color depth of your screen and the size and color depth at which you save the picture. You can substantially reduce the file size of a bitmap file (sometimes by more than 90 percent) by storing it in a compressed folder.

SEE ALSO: For information about compressed folders, see "Compressing Files" on page 132.

Editing a Picture

It's easy and fun to modify an existing bitmap picture to customize it, or to create a new picture using only part of the original picture. You can also modify the size or shape of part of the picture and can even create some special effects.

TIP: If you have a scanner or a digital camera set up on your computer, you can use the File menu to scan an image directly into Paint.

Crop a Picture

(1) Start Paint if it isn't already running.

(2) Scan or download an image into Paint, use the drawing tools to create a picture, or choose the Open command from the File menu to open an existing picture.

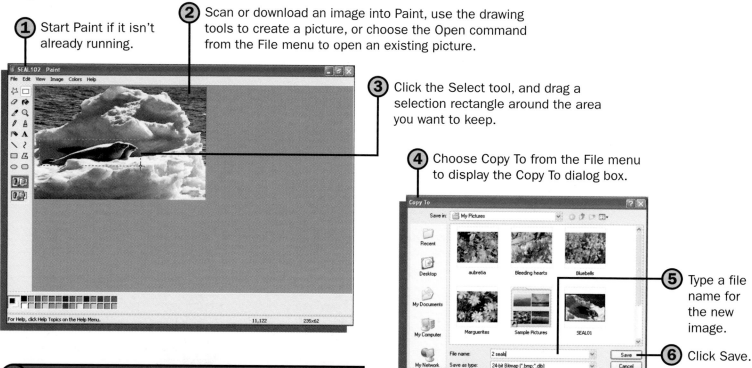

(3) Click the Select tool, and drag a selection rectangle around the area you want to keep.

(4) Choose Copy To from the File menu to display the Copy To dialog box.

(5) Type a file name for the new image.

(6) Click Save.

TRY THIS: Tweak your picture by clicking the Magnifier tool, selecting the 6x magnification level, and then using the Pencil tool to edit individual pixels, clicking the left mouse button for the foreground color and the right mouse button for the background color. Press Ctrl+G to display a grid identifying each pixel. Pres Ctrl+Page Up to return to Normal view.

TIP: You can save only the copied part of the picture as a bitmap (BMP) format. However, if you open the picture in Paint, you can then save it in a different format by choosing Save As from the File menu.

Modify a Picture's Size, Shape, or Color

① Use the Select tool to select the part of the picture you want to work on.

Hold down the Ctrl key and drag the selected picture to create a copy.

Drag a handle... ...to resize the selection.

② Modify the size or shape of the selection.

Hold down the Shift key and drag the selection to create a series of copies.

Choose a command from the Image menu to rotate the selection...

...or to reverse its colors...

...or to stretch and skew it.

③ Use the Eraser tool to delete part of the picture or to replace any color with the background color. To replace one color with another, set the foreground color to the color to be replaced and the background color to the replacement color, and then hold down the right mouse button and drag the Eraser over the area whose color you want to replace.

! TIP: To replace a large area with the background color, use the Select tool to select the area, and then press the Delete key.

! TIP: Don't forget the Undo command on the Edit menu. The first time you choose it, you undo your last action. You can choose the command again to undo the previous action and a third time to undo the action before that.

TRY THIS: Create a cropped picture. Open another picture in Paint, choose Paste From from the Edit menu, locate the cropped picture, and paste it into the second picture. Drag the inserted picture into the location you want, and click outside the selection. Save the edited picture.

Scanning a Picture

A scanner is a great tool for digitizing images and making them available on your computer. Windows XP provides access to your scanner with the Scanner And Camera Wizard, which steps you through the process. The wizard adapts to the specific features of your scanner, so the options you see in the wizard might be different from those described here. If you want to scan using a specific program, you can tell Windows XP to bypass the wizard and to automatically start the program you want when you press the scanner button.

Set Up a Picture

1 Choose Scanner And Camera Wizard from the Accessories submenu of the Start menu, and, if the Select Device dialog box appears, double-click your scanner. In the Scanner And Camera Wizard, click Next to start the wizard.

> **TIP:** You can also run the Scanner And Camera Wizard from the My Pictures folder by clicking Get Pictures From Camera Or Scanner in the Picture Tasks section of the window.

2 Specify the type of picture you're using.

3 Click Custom Settings if you want to change the picture's resolution, color intensity, or brightness.

5 Drag the handles in the preview to change the selected area if it doesn't include the part of the picture that you want.

4 Click Preview to do a quick scan of the picture and to preview it.

6 Click Next.

Scan the Picture

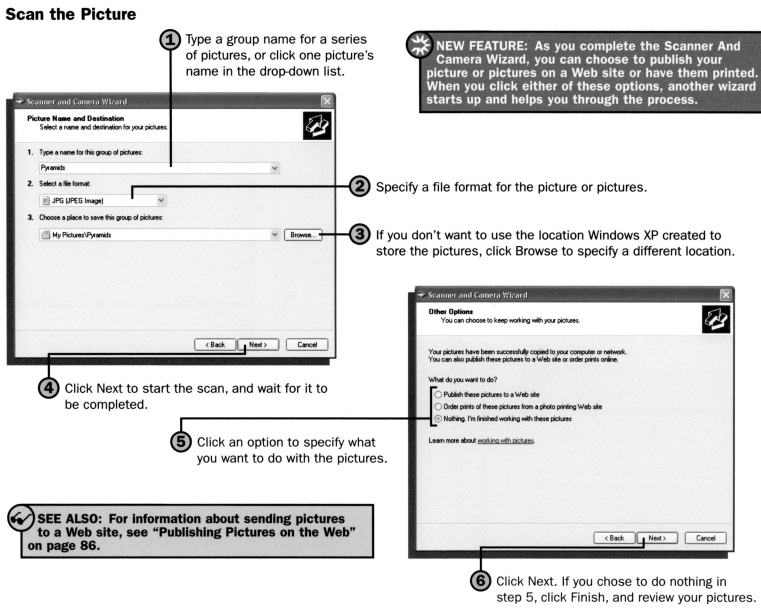

(1) Type a group name for a series of pictures, or click one picture's name in the drop-down list.

NEW FEATURE: As you complete the Scanner And Camera Wizard, you can choose to publish your picture or pictures on a Web site or have them printed. When you click either of these options, another wizard starts up and helps you through the process.

Scanner and Camera Wizard

Picture Name and Destination
Select a name and destination for your pictures.

1. Type a name for this group of pictures:

   Pyramids

2. Select a file format:

   JPG (JPEG Image)

(2) Specify a file format for the picture or pictures.

3. Choose a place to save this group of pictures:

   My Pictures\Pyramids   Browse...

(3) If you don't want to use the location Windows XP created to store the pictures, click Browse to specify a different location.

< Back   Next >   Cancel

(4) Click Next to start the scan, and wait for it to be completed.

Scanner and Camera Wizard

Other Options
You can choose to keep working with your pictures.

Your pictures have been successfully copied to your computer or network.
You can also publish these pictures to a Web site or order prints online.

What do you want to do?

○ Publish these pictures to a Web site
○ Order prints of these pictures from a photo printing Web site
⊙ Nothing. I'm finished working with these pictures

Learn more about working with pictures.

(5) Click an option to specify what you want to do with the pictures.

< Back   Next >   Cancel

SEE ALSO: For information about sending pictures to a Web site, see "Publishing Pictures on the Web" on page 86.

(6) Click Next. If you chose to do nothing in step 5, click Finish, and review your pictures.

Downloading Digital Camera Pictures

Once your digital camera is set up in Windows XP, the Scanner And Camera Wizard makes it easy for you to preview the pictures on your digital camera and to select the ones you want to download.

You can also specify where you want the pictures to be stored, how they're to be named, and whether you want them to be deleted from your camera after you've downloaded them.

Download Pictures

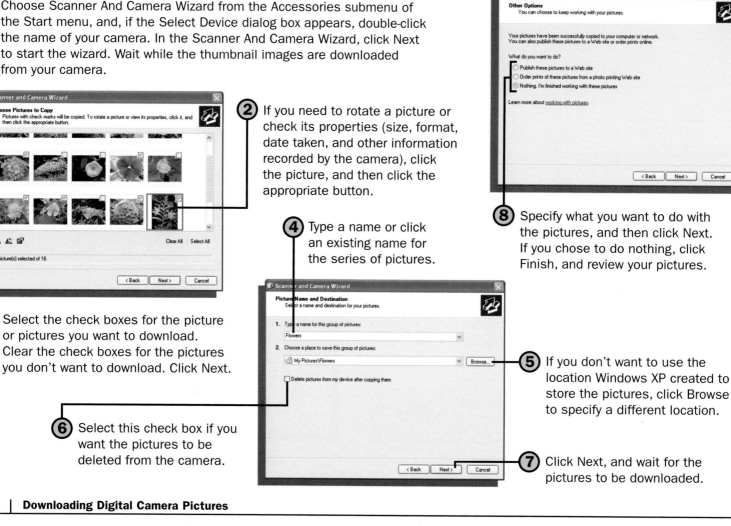

(1) Choose Scanner And Camera Wizard from the Accessories submenu of the Start menu, and, if the Select Device dialog box appears, double-click the name of your camera. In the Scanner And Camera Wizard, click Next to start the wizard. Wait while the thumbnail images are downloaded from your camera.

(2) If you need to rotate a picture or check its properties (size, format, date taken, and other information recorded by the camera), click the picture, and then click the appropriate button.

(3) Select the check boxes for the picture or pictures you want to download. Clear the check boxes for the pictures you don't want to download. Click Next.

(4) Type a name or click an existing name for the series of pictures.

(5) If you don't want to use the location Windows XP created to store the pictures, click Browse to specify a different location.

(6) Select this check box if you want the pictures to be deleted from the camera.

(7) Click Next, and wait for the pictures to be downloaded.

(8) Specify what you want to do with the pictures, and then click Next. If you chose to do nothing, click Finish, and review your pictures.

Manage the Camera and the Pictures

 Choose My Computer from the Start menu, and, in the My Computer window, double-click the name of your camera. Wait for information, including thumbnails of the pictures, to be downloaded. Click a picture, and specify what you want to do with it:

- Under File And Folder Tasks, click Publish This File To The Web to use the Web Publishing Wizard to place a picture on a Web site.

- Under File And Folder Tasks, click Delete This File to delete a picture from the camera without downloading it.

- Double-click a file to see a large preview of the picture. Use the tools in the Windows Picture And Fax Viewer, where the picture is displayed, to print, copy, or view the picture. Close the window when you've finished.

- Right-click a picture, and choose Save In My Pictures from the shortcut menu to save the picture file to the My Pictures folder.

- Under Camera Tasks, click Delete All Pictures On Camera to delete all the pictures in the camera without downloading them.

② Click Show Camera Properties to see and modify the camera settings and to conduct a diagnostic test of the camera.

> **! TIP:** If Windows XP doesn't automatically set up the camera when it's first connected, use the manufacturer's setup disk to install it. You can also manually install your camera by clicking Printers And Other Hardware in the Control Panel and then clicking Scanners And Cameras. Use the Add An Imaging Device option in the Imaging Tasks section to install the camera.

> **✋ CAUTION:** Until you've completed the wizard, only small thumbnail images of your pictures have been sent to your computer; the pictures themselves still reside only in your camera.

> **⊘ SEE ALSO:** For information about renaming files, see "Rename a File" and "Rename a Group of Files" on page 127.

> **! TIP:** Switch to Details view to see the picture format, the date the picture was taken, and the size of the file. You'll see a preview of the selected picture in the Details part of the window.

Viewing Pictures

Windows XP provides a variety of ways to view your pictures so that you can decide which ones to keep, copy, print, or send to friends.

View All the Pictures

(1) In the folder that contains the pictures, click the Views button, and click Filmstrip in the list if it isn't already selected.

(2) Click a picture to see it in an enlarged size.

(5) To view all the pictures in the folder as full-screen images, click View As A Slide Show.

(6) To advance a picture before it would normally advance, click anywhere in the picture.

(7) To control the slide show, move the mouse to display the controls, and then use them to pause, advance, repeat, or end the slide show.

(3) To view the pictures in sequence, click the Next Image button (or press the Right arrow key); to go through the pictures in reverse order, click the Previous Image button (or press the Left arrow key).

(4) To rotate a picture, click the Rotate Clockwise or the Rotate Counterclockwise button.

> **SEE ALSO:** For information about e-mailing your pictures, see "Sending or Receiving a File" on page 58.
>
> For information about printing your pictures, see "Printing Your Photographs" on page 116.

Preview a Single Picture

(1) In the folder window containing your pictures, double-click a picture to display it in the Windows Picture And Fax Viewer.

(2) Use the controls on the toolbar to change the view of the picture; to rotate it; or to edit, copy, or print it.

(3) Close the window when you've finished.

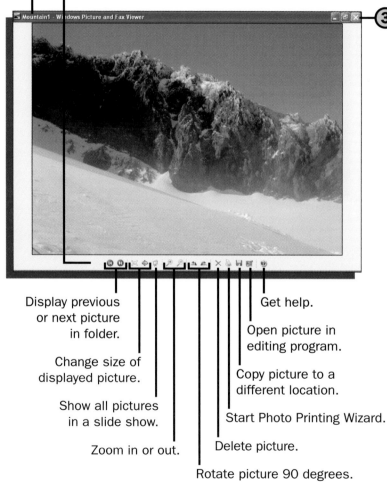

Mountain1 - Windows Picture and Fax Viewer

Display previous or next picture in folder.

Change size of displayed picture.

Show all pictures in a slide show.

Zoom in or out.

Rotate picture 90 degrees.

Delete picture.

Start Photo Printing Wizard.

Copy picture to a different location.

Open picture in editing program.

Get help.

> **! TIP:** Choose Tiles from the Views button to see a listing of your pictures that includes information about the dimensions of each picture (in pixels) and its file type. Choose Details from the Views button to see the size of the file, the date each picture was taken, and the date the file was last modified.

> **! TIP:** When you click the button on the Windows Picture And Fax Viewer toolbar that opens the picture for editing, the picture will open in Paint unless you have another picture-editing program installed.

> **! TIP:** When you're in Filmstrip view, double-click a thumbnail picture instead of the preview picture to display the picture in the Windows Picture And Fax Viewer.

> **! TIP:** If your picture is in the TIF format, some annotation buttons are also available. These buttons are used primarily for annotating faxes that are in the TIF format.

> **SEE ALSO:** For information about editing a picture in Paint, see "Editing a Picture" on page 78.
>
> For information about working with faxes, see "Sending a Fax" on page 118, "Receiving a Fax" on page 120, "Reviewing a Fax You've Received" on page 121, and "Viewing and Annotating a Fax" on page 122.

Publishing Pictures on the Web ⊛ NEW FEATURE

When you have some great pictures, you almost always want to share them with family, friends, or colleagues. One of the best ways to do this is to *publish* the pictures by putting them up on a Web site. Then you can let people know where to find the pictures so that they can view them at their leisure. Note that this procedure is based on using MSN (The Microsoft Network). If you're using another provider, the procedure might vary slightly.

Publish Your Pictures

(1) In the folder that contains your pictures, select the picture you want to publish. If you want to publish multiple pictures, make sure they're all in the same folder (but you don't need to select them at this point).

(2) Click Publish This File To The Web to start the Web Publishing Wizard, and click Next to enter the wizard.

(5) Specify the resolution you want for the pictures. (The higher the resolution, the longer it will take for you to upload the pictures and for those who view them to download them.)

(6) Click Next to upload the pictures, and then click Finish to complete the wizard.

(3) Select the check boxes for the pictures you want to publish, and clear the check boxes for the pictures you don't want to publish.

(4) Click Next, and step through the wizard, providing the following information:

- The service provider you want to use
- Whether the pictures (and the folder containing the pictures) are to be available to the public or only to the people you specify
- Whether you want to use an existing Web account or create a new one
- The folder in which you want to store the pictures

Recording a Video Clip

With Windows Movie Maker, you can create a digital video file from a video camera, from a videotape, or from television—provided you have the proper equipment. To record from a digital video camera or VCR, the device must be connected to your computer through an IEEE 1394 card. To record from an analog video camera or VCR, you need a video-capture card or some other device to convert images from analog to digital. If you're using a digital Web camera, you simply need to have the camera hooked up directly to your computer. After you've created the video clip, you can play it as is or combine it with other video and audio clips to make a movie.

> **!** **TIP: If you're using a digital camera or VCR, the Record dialog box will also include play controls that you can use to control the camera or the VCR. When the part of the video you want to record is playing, click Record. After you've finished recording, click the Stop button to stop the camera or the VCR.**

Record a Video Clip

1 Start Movie Maker from the Accessories submenu of the Start menu, and click Record to display the Record dialog box.

2 Specify the type of recording.

3 If you have multiple video input devices and you want to change the device or the audio source you'll be using, click Change Device, and specify another device or audio source.

4 To limit the length of the recording, select this check box, and specify the maximum time you want to allow for the clip.

5 If you want Movie Maker to automatically create separate clips of your recording when it detects a completely different set of frames, select this check box. Clear the check box if you want to create a single clip.

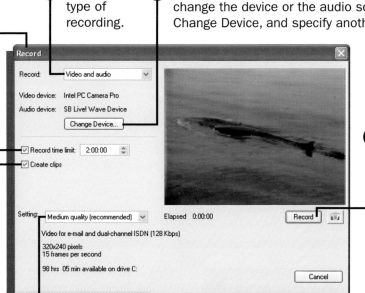

7 Start your playback from the camera or VCR, or the live recording from the camera. When you reach the content you want to record, click Record. After you've recorded all the content you want, click Stop. In the Save Windows Media File dialog box that appears, type a name for the file, and click OK.

6 Specify the quality of the recording. (The higher the quality, the larger the file that will be created.) Click Other in the list to specify a very high level of recording.

Making a Movie

You can create and edit digital movies with Movie Maker, and, because Movie Maker compresses the files, your movies can be small enough to include with your e-mail. You movie can be composed of all or part of a single video file, or it can be a composite of parts of different video files.

Gather Your Resources

1 Start Movie Maker from the Accessories submenu of the Start menu.

SEE ALSO: For information about recording video clips, see "Recording a Video Clip" on page 87.

For information about editing clips or adding transition effects between clips, see "Editing Your Movie" on page 90.

For information about adding narration or a soundtrack to your movie, see "Adding Audio to Your Movie" on page 92.

For information about including digital still pictures in your movie, see "Adding Slides to a Movie" on page 96.

2 If you want to import a video file from another source, choose Import from the File menu, and, in the Select File To Import dialog box, locate and select the video file you want. Click Open.

4 Click a file to see the clips it contains.

3 If you haven't recorded your videos, click Record, and record them.

5 Double-click a video clip to preview it.

6 If you want to create two clips from one clip, play the clip up to the point where you want to separate it, click Pause, drag the slider to move to the frame where you want to split the clip, and click the Split Clip button.

Split Clip button

7 Continue reviewing the clips that are contained in your video files, noting the ones you want to use and the order in which you want them to appear in your movie.

CAUTION: To record a movie, your computer should have at least a 300 MHz Pentium II processor, 64 MB of RAM, and 2 GB of free disk space. To record from a digital camera or a digital VCR, your computer should have at least a 600 MHz Pentium III processor and 128 MB of RAM.

Create a Movie

① Select the first video clip to be shown in the movie.

④ When you've assembled all the clips and the movie is just the way you want it, click Save Movie.

⑤ Specify the Playback quality, and note the way different quality settings affect the time it takes to download the movie.

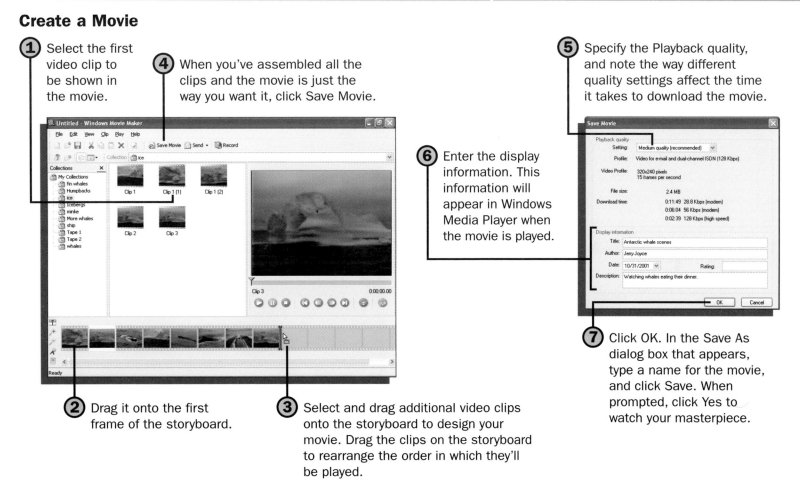

⑥ Enter the display information. This information will appear in Windows Media Player when the movie is played.

② Drag it onto the first frame of the storyboard.

③ Select and drag additional video clips onto the storyboard to design your movie. Drag the clips on the storyboard to rearrange the order in which they'll be played.

⑦ Click OK. In the Save As dialog box that appears, type a name for the movie, and click Save. When prompted, click Yes to watch your masterpiece.

⚠ **TIP:** You aren't limited to the clips from a single video file. To add a video clip from a different file, click the file in the Collections pane, and use the clips in that file.

⚠ **TIP:** You can't save the movie project until you've added at least one clip to the storyboard. Don't forget to save the project frequently so that you can always return to it to modify your movie.

Editing Your Movie

After you've created a movie using Movie Maker, you can modify your movie by cropping to include only part of a clip, creating fade-in/fade-out transitions between clips, adding a background sound clip, or recording a narration.

 TIP: The part of the clip that you trim away isn't deleted—it's just hidden. To restore the entire clip, select it, and choose Clear Trim Points from the Clip menu.

Crop a Clip

(1) Start Movie Maker from the Accessories submenu of the Start menu, and use the Open Project button to open your existing movie project if it isn't already open.

(4) Choose Set Start Trim Point from the Clip menu.

(6) Choose Set End Trim Point from the Clip menu.

(2) Select the clip you want to crop.

(3) Drag the Seek Bar to the point where you want to start the clip.

(5) Drag the Seek Bar to the point where you want to end the clip.

Create a Transition

(1) Choose Timeline from the View menu.

(4) When everything is perfect, save your movie, and preview it.

(5) Save the project, and close Movie Maker.

TIP: You can modify the trim points of a clip in Timeline view by selecting the clip and dragging the triangular clip markers at the top of the timeline.

TIP: Use the Zoom In or Zoom Out button on the timeline to change the scale of the timeline for easier manipulation of clip transitions or cropping.

TIP: To quickly change between Storyboard and Timeline views, click the Timeline button at the left of the storyboard or click the Storyboard button at the left of the timeline.

(3) Drag the left border of the clip onto the clip at the left. The farther you drag the clip, the longer the transition. Repeat with any other clips between which you want to create transitions.

(2) Click the clip that you want to fade into. (It's at the right of the clip that you want to fade out of.)

TRY THIS: Assemble your clips on the storyboard, and crop them as desired. Switch to Timeline view, and drag the left border of a clip onto the clip at the left. Create additional transitions. Click at the beginning of the timeline, and then click the Play button to preview the effects. Change any trim point or transition that's not to your liking.

Adding Audio to Your Movie

When you record a movie with Movie Maker, you can record an
audio track at the same time. If you didn't record a track, however,
and you want to add one now, or if you want to add a narration or
a musical soundtrack to an existing movie, it's a simple process.
A narration can either merge with the existing audio for the movie
or completely replace it, whereas a soundtrack is always merged
with any existing audio for the movie.

> **! TIP: A narration file is a WAV-type file, not a Windows
> Media Format file. When you add a narration file to
> a movie, the file's content is incorporated into the
> movie's Windows Media File format.**

Create a Narration

3 Click the Record Narration
button to display the Record
Narration Track dialog box.

1 Start Windows Movie Maker
from the Accessories
submenu of the Start menu,
and use the Open Project
button to open your
existing movie project if it
isn't already open. Make
sure that all your video
clips are in place and
in the correct order.

4 Confirm that the correct
recording source is dis-
played. If you want to use
a different source, click the
Change button, and specify
the recording source.

2 Click the Timeline
button if the timeline
isn't displayed.

6 Set the Record Level. Speak
into your microphone and
use the gauge to determine
the proper level. You can
also adjust the level while
you're recording.

Record Narration button —

5 Select the Mute Video Soundtrack check box if you want
to omit a sound track that was recorded with the video clip
and replace it with your narration, or clear the check box to
merge the narration with the audio for the video. (The check
box might be grayed and unavailable, depending on the type
of recording and the equipment installed on your computer.)

7 Click Record. Watch your movie in the preview window
and on the timeline as you record your narration. When
you've finished, click the Stop button (the Record button
changes into the Stop button after you click Record),
and save the narration file to a folder. The narration is
automatically placed in the audio portion of the timeline.

Add a Soundtrack

1 Create or import the audio files that you want to use for your soundtrack. The files need not be in Windows Media Format, but neither can they be protected media such as some CD music. You'll probably need to experiment to see which types of audio files you can use.

3 Choose Play Entire Storyboard/Timeline from the Play menu to preview your movie.

4 If the video and audio are arranged to your satisfaction, click Save Movie to create your movie. Close Movie Maker when you've finished.

2 Drag a sound clip onto the audio bar at the location (that is, the time) where you want the clip to be played during the movie. Add and position any other sound clips.

SEE ALSO: For information about saving CD music to your hard drive in Windows Media Format, see "Copying CD Music" on page 100.

For information about recording your own sound files, see "Creating a Sound File" on page 107 and "Creating an Audio Clip" on page 108.

CAUTION: If you're using music from a CD or another similar source for your soundtrack, be careful not to violate the copyright of the material.

Making Movies that People Actually Enjoy

We all love our own home movies, and, because we're usually reliving happy times when we watch them, we're tolerant of their flaws. Before we ask anyone else to watch a home movie, though, we should try to improve it as much as possible so that the members of our captive audience actually enjoy the show rather than squirming with embarrassment or trying to hide their yawning boredom. The trick, of course, is to use good camera skills so that you avoid the most common problems—for example, panning and zooming too fast or too slowly, jittery pictures, bad lighting, and poorly composed images. However, once you've recorded your movie, there are several ways you can improve it if you need to.

Edit Your Movie

Even world-famous directors and experienced camera operators don't make a perfect movie as they're filming it. That's where the movie editor comes in!

Take out the trash. Don't use any material of inferior quality. You might love a clip that brings back fond memories even though Uncle David's head is cut off, but your audience won't love it. You can easily delete the substandard material by splitting the clip, separating the quality from the trash, and using only the best clips. For information about previewing and splitting clips, see "Gather Your Resources" on page 88.

Arrange the content. You don't have to keep your movie's scenes in the order in which they were shot. Be creative. You might want to rearrange the clips based on subject matter or to produce a more logical sequence of events. Pay attention to continuity—for example, don't jump from a glimpse of Auntie Mimi presiding over a sunny picnic to an unrelated shot of her on a rainy day inside and then back to the same sunny picnic just because you didn't have enough footage of her at the picnic.

Tighten up the scenes. When you review the assembled movie and find that a scene runs too long, you'll probably want to crop it down to prevent your audience's attention from wandering. You can easily crop the beginning or the end of a clip by setting crop marks in the clip. For information about cropping a clip, see "Crop a Clip" on page 90.

Control narrations and soundtracks. These elements can add a great deal of sophistication to a movie, but you need to insert them carefully. The sound content must be closely coordinated with the video action, and the sound quality and volume should add to rather than distract from the subject matter of the movie. If you're going to add a narration, write a script first, and rehearse it as often as you need to while you're previewing the movie. When you're sure the narration works, use a good-quality microphone to record it. Whether you're using a narration or a soundtrack, make sure the volume is adjusted properly so that it doesn't either get lost among the background sounds or blast your viewers out of their seats.

Check with the reviewers. Don't trust yourself to be objective about your movie. Before you distribute it, ask at least one person whose opinion you value to review the movie and to give you some constructive criticism. Then, if you need to, you can go back to your video project and make some tweaks to produce a movie that will leave your audience eager to watch your next extravaganza.

Make It Available

The size of your movie plays a large part in the way you're going to distribute it. If you create a huge video file, you shouldn't expect people to receive it by e-mail or to wait forever as they download it from the Web. Of course, if you're going to distribute your movie in some other way, you might want to maximize the quality of the video and disregard the file size.

Use the appropriate quality. In a video file, the quality of the video is directly proportional to the file size. Decide how you're going to distribute your movie, and set the quality for that distribution mode. In the Save Movie dialog box, you can see just how the various quality settings will affect download time. Consider creating several versions of the movie, using different playback-quality settings for different ways of distributing the movie.

Post it on the Web. You can use a Web service that lets you publish your movie on the Web so that other people can play it directly from the Web site. To post your video on one of these services, in Movie Maker, point to Send Movie To on the File menu, and choose Web Server from the submenu.

E-mail it. You can e-mail your movie in two different ways. To e-mail it directly from Movie Maker, point to Send Movie To on the File menu, and choose E-Mail from the submenu. This is an especially useful way to e-mail early versions of your movie out for review. To e-mail the final version of your video, save the movie, and, in the My Videos folder (assuming that's where you store your videos), select the video file, and click E-Mail This File in the Files And Folder Tasks section of the window.

Put it on a CD. If you've created a large video file because of very high-quality recording and playback settings and/or lots of content, and if you have a CD recorder on your computer, you can put the video on a CD and distribute the CD. To do so, save the movie, and, in the My Videos folder, select the video file, and click Copy To CD in the Video Tasks section of the window.

Know the format. Your video files are in Windows Media Format (except for some high-quality recordings from a digital source, which, depending on your settings, might be in the AVI format). Windows Media Format files require Windows Media Player, so verify that whoever is going to view your video has that player installed.

Going Further

Windows Movie Maker is a great tool for making home movies. If you want to explore moviemaking in greater depth, however, you can purchase other programs that provide more power and complexity. You can also visit the Microsoft Windows Media Web page at *www.microsoft.com/windows/windowsmedia*. There you'll find more advanced moviemaking programs and free utilities to modify your video files or to convert them into other formats, as well as software to encode them, which can dramatically reduce file size.

Adding Slides to a Movie

Your movie doesn't have to be all action. You can add digital pictures—photographs from a digital camera, for example—to your video clips to create title slides or still photographs to supplement the video clips. Or you can create a movie file using your still pictures and some music to produce a slide show with an accompanying soundtrack. You can also edit pictures or create them from scratch to add title slides for your movie.

Add Slides

1 Start Movie Maker from the Accessories submenu of the Start menu.

2 Click New Collections, and name a new collections folder for the pictures.

3 Import pictures into the new folder you just created. Choose Import from the File menu, locate and select the pictures to be used, and click Open. (To select multiple pictures, hold down the Ctrl key and click each picture you want.)

4 Choose Options from the View menu to display the Options dialog box, and specify the length of time you want each picture to be displayed. Click OK.

6 Click Save Movie when you've finished.

5 Drag the pictures onto the storyboard in the sequence in which you want them displayed. Use the Timeline view to add any audio or transition effects, or to modify the length of time an individual picture is displayed.

> **TRY THIS:** Open a picture in Paint, and use the **Stretch/Skew** command on the Image menu to shrink the picture to a size of approximately **320 x 240 pixels. Choose Draw Opaque** from the Image menu if the command has a check mark next to it. Use the Text tool to insert the text of a title slide in the font and color you want. Save the picture using a different name, and then import the picture into Movie Maker.

Working with Music, Voice, and Sounds

If you like music, you'll *love* Microsoft Windows Media Player because of the freedom it gives you to control and customize the music you want to hear. You can use Media Player to download from the Internet all sorts of information about your favorite albums or performers, to play music tracks, and to copy individual pieces of music or entire CDs to your computer. You can arrange the media you want to play, regardless of format—songs, video clips, and so on—in the order you want in your own customized *playlist*. If your computer is equipped with a CD recorder, you can record individual tracks to create your own CD. And it's a lot of fun to choose among dozens of cool designs to outfit Media Player with a new *skin* to drastically transform its appearance.

Using Sound Recorder, you can record spoken messages or the music or sounds of your choice, mainly for use on your own computer. A more sophisticated method of recording is to use Windows Movie Maker to record an audio clip. You're not limited as to the length of your recording, you can record individual tracks or complete CDs, and Windows Media Format can compress the files for maximum portability.

Microsoft Windows XP provides another form of sound in a program called Narrator that actually reads aloud to you. Provided your computer has a sound system, Narrator's voice can describe the items on your screen and can read blocks of text to you. Whether you use Narrator for the sheer novelty of it or because you find it difficult or tiring to read from the screen, it's worth trying. You can even adjust the speed, volume, and pitch of Narrator's voice for your individual listening pleasure.

Playing a Music CD

Playing a CD is as simple as putting the CD into the drive and waiting for Windows Media Player to start playing the music. However, Media Player can also provide additional information from the Internet about the music and the performer. With or without this additional information, you can control and customize the way the music is played.

Play a CD

(1) If you want to download information about an album, connect to the Internet before you play the CD. Insert the CD into the disc drive. If the Audio CD dialog box appears, click the Play Audio CD option if it isn't already selected, and click OK. Wait for Windows Media Player to start playing the CD.

(9) Click the AutoHide Menu Bar button to hide or show the full window and menu bar.

(8) Click the Hide Taskbar button to hide or show the taskbar.

(7) Use the Visualization buttons to change the display.

(6) Use the Select View button to cycle through the different settings you can make.

! **TIP: To always open a music CD in Windows Media Player if the Audio CD dialog box appears, select the Always Do The Selected Action check box before you click OK. If the Audio CD dialog box doesn't appear, and if Media Player doesn't start automatically, choose Windows Media Player from the All Programs submenu of the Start menu, click the name of the CD in the Playlist, and click OK.**

! **TIP: The album information is provided for your convenience. If you don't download the information (or if the album isn't listed in the database), the name of the album will be listed as Unknown Artist and the tracks as Track 1, Track 2, and so on. You can edit a track name by right-clicking it and choosing Edit from the shortcut menu.**

(2) Click the Show Equalizer And Setting button if the Equalizer isn't displayed. Use the Equalizer buttons to modify the playback.

(3) Click the Show Playlist button if the playlist isn't displayed.

(4) Double-click a track in the playlist to jump to that track.

(5) Use the buttons and sliders to control the play and the volume just as you would on any CD player.

Changing Media Player's Skin

You can change Media Player's appearance by viewing it in Full Mode or Skin Mode, and by changing its skin. Skins are designs that alter the appearance—but not the functionality—of Media Player. You use skins only when Media Player is in Skin Mode, but it's quick and easy to switch between the two modes whenever you want.

Change Its Skin

! **TIP: Media Player will have additional controls if your computer is set up to play DVD movies.**

① If Media Player isn't already running, start it from the All Programs submenu of the Start menu.

④ Click Apply Skin.

③ Click a design in the list.

② Click the Skin Chooser tab.

⑥ To return to the normal display, click the Return To Full Mode button. If you click the Switch To Skin Mode button while Media Player is in Full Mode, you'll be switched back to Skin Mode and the previously selected skin.

⑤ Use the controls to play the media.

Switch To Skin Mode button

Minimize button
Close button
Volume button
Open Playlist button
Pause button
Open Graphic Equalizer button

Mute button
Rewind button
Fast Forward button
Seek button
Previous button
Play/Stop button
Next button

! **TIP: You can download additional skins by clicking the More Skins button on the Skin Chooser tab. Custom skins are also available from many music Web sites. Microsoft Plus! For Windows provides even more skins and visualizations, plus several utilities, for Media Player.**

Copying CD Music

Instead of playing a different CD every time you want to hear a particular song or piece of music, you can copy individual tunes or entire CDs onto your computer's hard disk; then you can play the saved music in any order you like. When you copy the music, it's saved in Windows Media Format, which takes about half as much space as the original CD format and which allows you to transfer the music to another device—a portable player or a hand-held computer, for example. You can also record the saved music onto a CD if your computer is equipped with a CD recorder.

Copy the Music

1 If you want to download information about an album, connect to the Internet. If Media Player isn't already running, start it from the All Programs submenu of the Start menu. Make sure the CD you want to copy is in the CD drive.

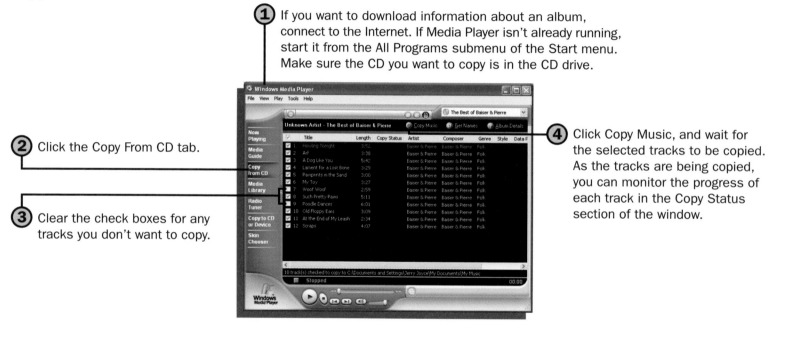

2 Click the Copy From CD tab.

3 Clear the check boxes for any tracks you don't want to copy.

4 Click Copy Music, and wait for the selected tracks to be copied. As the tracks are being copied, you can monitor the progress of each track in the Copy Status section of the window.

> **!** **TIP:** To play copied music, on the Now Playing tab, with the Playlist displayed, click the category of the music you want to hear, and then double-click a specific track in the playlist.

> **!** **TIP:** If you didn't download the names of the tracks before getting ready to copy them, make sure that you're connected to the Internet, and then click the Get Names button to search the Internet for the details.

Create a Music CD ⊕ NEW FEATURE

② Select the music genre, album, playlist, or track that contains the music to be copied.

① Click the Copy To CD Or Device tab. Make sure you have a blank CD in your CD recorder.

③ Select the check boxes for the tracks you want to copy, and clear the check boxes for the tracks you don't want to copy.

⑤ Click the Copy Music button (the button changes to Cancel as soon as you start copying), and wait for the files to be converted and copied.

④ If you have more than one recording device, specify the device you want to use.

✋ **CAUTION: Most CD music is protected by a license.** When you copy a piece of music from a CD, Media Player searches the Internet for the appropriate license and transfers it to your computer. Depending on the terms of the license, you might or might not be able to download the saved music to a portable player or a different computer. If you can't connect to the Internet or if Media Player can't access a license for you, choose Options from the Tools menu, and, on the Copy Music tab, select the Protect Content check box to have a license issued as you copy the music. This license allows you to copy the music to your hard disk, to a portable device, or to another CD. If you copy music without a license, you could be violating the music's copyright.

❗ **TIP: To adjust the quality of your CD recordings, and thus the amount of space each track occupies on the CD, choose Options from the Tools menu, and make your changes on the Copy Music tab.**

❗ **TIP: You can also use the procedure described here to copy music to a portable device. To manage your recording devices, choose Options from the Tools menu, and click the Devices tab.**

👓 **SEE ALSO: For information about creating a playlist so that you can record a CD from a variety of sources, see "Playing Media Using a Playlist" on page 103.**

Playing a Saved Media File

Media Player makes it easy to play audio or video files that you've saved on your computer, that are stored somewhere on your network, or that reside on a Web page on the Internet. The files are listed by category for easy access, regardless of where they're stored.

 SEE ALSO: For information about creating a personal playlist that preprograms the items to be played, see "Playing Media Using a Playlist" on the facing page.

Start Playing

1 If Media Player isn't already running, start it from the All Programs submenu of the Start menu.

2 Click the Media Library tab.

4 Double-click the track to play it. If you want, you can switch to the Now Playing tab to watch the track being played.

3 Specify a category and a subcategory to locate the track you want to play. If the track isn't in the list, you can locate it by pressing Ctrl+E and searching your computer for all media files.

TIP: To add to the Media Library every track that you play, regardless of its location, choose Options from the Tools menu, and, on the Player tab, select the check boxes for adding items that you've played. Click OK. To manually add an item, click the Add To Library button on the Media Library tab, and choose what you want to add from the menu.

TIP: Media Player can play music files, video files, and DVD files. You can also use it to view the Windowsmedia Web page for information and links to other music Web sites, to download or play music and videos, and to listen to radio stations over the Internet.

Playing Media Using a Playlist

A playlist is a list of media files and their locations that you can use to organize your music, your videos, and any other multimedia files and locations for easy access and play. When you use your playlist, the items in it, regardless of their format and location, are played in the order you specify.

TRY THIS: Open the My Music folder, locate a track you want to add to your playlist, right-click the track, and choose Add To Playlist from the shortcut menu. Click the playlist, and then click OK.

Create a Playlist

(2) Click New Playlist.

(5) Click Add To Playlist, and click the newly created playlist to add the selected item or items to the list. Repeat to add other items to the playlist.

(1) If Media Player isn't already running, start it from the All Programs submenu of the Start menu, and click the Media Library tab.

(6) Click the playlist to play the items in the list. Switch to the Now Playing tab to see all the items in the playlist.

(4) Click to select an item, or hold down the Ctrl key and click to select multiple items in any Media Library category that you want to add to your playlist.

(3) In the New Playlist dialog box that appears, type a name for the playlist, and click OK.

TIP: To change the order of the items in your playlist, go to the Media Library, click the playlist, click the item you want to move, and use the Move Up or Move Down button to rearrange the order of the list. To delete an item, click the Delete button, and choose the action you want from the menu.

Controlling the Volume

If the sound your computer emits to signal an event—the logon or logoff sound, for example—is an earsplitting assault, relief in the form of adjusting the volume is just a click away. You can also use the Volume Control to keep your music and other sounds muted so that you don't disturb other people, or, when you're the only person around, you can crank up the sound level and blast away! You can also control the volume levels when you're using a microphone or any input line and can select the best settings for your speakers. Although many programs have individual controls, you can use the Volume Control to set all your sound levels.

! TIP: If the Volume icon doesn't appear on the taskbar, choose Control Panel from the Start menu, and click the Sounds, Speech, And Audio Devices category. Click the Adjust The System Volume task, and, on the Volume tab, select the Place Volume Icon In The Taskbar check box. Click OK. If the icon still doesn't appear on the taskbar, your sound system might not work with this control. Instead, use the controls on the Volume tab of the Sounds And Audio Devices Properties dialog box.

Set the Master Volume Level

Show Hidden
Icons button

3 Click outside the Volume icon to close it.

2 Drag the slider to adjust the volume.

1 Click the Volume icon in the notification area of the taskbar. If Windows has hidden infrequently used icons in the notification area so that the Volume icon isn't visible, click the Show Hidden Icons button.

! TIP: If you're using a device that isn't listed in the Volume Control, choose Properties from the Options menu, and select the check box for the device. To see any available advanced settings, including tone settings, and using only digital sound output, choose Advanced Options from the Options menu, and then click any Advanced button that you see in the Volume Control.

Set the Volume for Individual Devices

1 Double-click the Volume icon on the taskbar.

2 Adjust the settings for the device or devices whose volume you want to adjust, and then use the device or devices to check the sound level.

3 When the adjustments are correct, close the Volume Control.

Set the Recording Volume

1 Double-click the Volume icon on the taskbar.

2 Choose Properties from the Options menu to display the Properties dialog box, and click the Recording option.

3 Select the check boxes for the devices to be displayed in the Recording Control, and clear the check boxes for the devices you don't want displayed. Click OK.

! TIP: The items listed in the Show The Following Volume Controls list in the Properties dialog box depend on your computer's sound system and on the equipment installed on the computer.

✋ CAUTION: Before you spend a lot of time trying to tweak your volume settings, make sure that you have the correct settings for your speakers. To see whether the speakers have been set up with the correct configuration, choose Control Panel from the Start menu, and click the Sounds, Speech, And Audio Devices category. Click the Change The Speaker Settings task. Under Speaker Settings, click Advanced, and then specify the correct speaker configuration in the list. Click OK, click the Speaker Volume button, adjust the speakers, and then click OK in the Speaker Volume dialog box and again in the Sound And Audio Devices Properties dialog box.

4 Adjust the settings for the device or devices whose recording volume you want to adjust, and then use the device or devices to check the sound level.

5 When the adjustments are correct, close the Recording Control.

Letting Your Computer Do the Talking

Windows XP provides a program called Narrator that actually speaks to you! Narrator can describe aloud the items that are currently displayed on your screen, and it can even read long blocks of text. Narrator has some limitations, but it can be very useful in the right circumstances. Of course, for Narrator to work, your computer must have a sound system.

> **(!) TIP:** Some programs, such as Microsoft Office XP, have much greater voice capabilities than Narrator, including full voice recognition. If you have installed any such programs, you might find different settings for Narrator from those described here. To view all the settings, open the Control Panel from the Start menu; click the Sounds, Speech, And Audio Devices icon; and then click the Speech icon.

Listen to Narrator

(1) Choose Narrator from the Accessibilities submenu of the Start menu to display the Narrator dialog box. If you see an introductory dialog box, click OK.

(2) Select this check box to have Narrator describe aloud all the elements in the active window, the items on the Desktop, and so on.

(3) Select this check box to have Narrator read aloud any editable text, such as text in a WordPad document.

(4) Select this check box to have the mouse pointer move automatically to the item that's active or currently selected.

(5) Select this check box to have the Narrator dialog box minimized and out of the way when you start Narrator.

(8) Click the Minimize button when you've adjusted all the settings to your satisfaction.

(9) To close Narrator, click its button on the taskbar to restore it if you've minimized it, and then click Exit.

(6) Click Voice to open the Voice Settings dialog box.

(7) Adjust the reading speed, volume, and pitch of Narrator's voice. Click OK when you've finished.

> **TRY THIS:** Start Narrator, and select the Read Typed Characters check box. Open an existing WordPad document, preferably one that contains a lot of text. Listen as Narrator reads the text. Switch to various other programs to determine which ones Narrator can or can't read from.

Creating a Sound File

You usually use a sound file to record or play a short, simple sound—a beep or a bark, an occasional musical chord or two, or even a short message. Windows XP and many programs use sound files (called *WAV files*) to mark an event—starting up, for example—or to record a short message, such as an audio comment. Using Sound Recorder and a microphone or some other input device, you can record and play your own sound files, each of which can be up to 60 seconds long.

> **TIP:** To reduce the size of a sound file, save the file, choose Properties from the File menu, and choose a format that will compress the sound file. Different formats are designed for different purposes, so take a look at the Sound Recorder Help file if you need information about the various formats.

Record Sounds

1 Choose Sound Recorder from the Entertainment submenu of the Start menu.

2 Click the Record button, and record the sounds you want.

3 Click Stop when you've finished.

4 Choose Save from the File menu, and save the file.

> **TIP:** The Stop button is grayed and inactive until you start recording.

> **SEE ALSO:** For Information about setting the recording levels for different input devices, see "Set the Recording Volume" on page 105.
>
> For information about recording audio files in Windows Media Format, see "Creating an Audio Clip" on page 108.

Add Sounds and Effects

1 Move the slider to the location in the sound file where you want to add an existing sound file.

2 From the Edit menu, choose Insert File to add a file and to record over any existing sound, or choose Mix With File to merge a file with any existing sound. Use either the Insert File or the Merge With File dialog box to locate the file you want, and click Open.

4 Choose Save from the File menu.

3 From the Effects menu, choose the type of effect you want to add to the entire sound file:

- Increase Volume or Decrease Volume to change the volume of the recorded file
- Increase Speed or Decrease Speed to speed up or slow down the recording
- Add Echo to add an echo to the recording
- Reverse to have the recording play backward

Creating an Audio Clip

An audio clip is a file in Windows Media Format that contains only audio. You can record a single audio clip using a microphone or any other input device attached to your computer. You can also combine an existing Windows Media Format audio file with a larger audio file, or you can convert into Windows Media Format an audio file that was recorded in a different format.

> ! **TIP:** You can record from different devices by attaching them to the Line In connection on your computer's sound card or sound system. However, unless you have a really good sound system, any recordings you make using the Line In connection will not be of a very high quality. You can also record from a CD playing in your computer's CD drive.

Record an Audio Clip

1 Start Movie Maker from the Accessories submenu of the Start menu. If necessary, start a new project, and create a new collection to hold your audio clips. Click Record to display the Record dialog box.

2 Click Audio Only in the list.

3 If the correct source of the audio isn't listed, click Change Device, specify the device you want, and click OK.

4 Specify the quality you want for the recording. Click Other in the list if you want to see an additional list in which you can specify further levels of recording quality.

5 Click Record, and record your audio. When you've finished, click Stop, and save the file. (Note that the Record button changes into the Stop button as soon as you start recording.)

> ✋ **CAUTION:** Be careful not to violate copyright laws and licenses when you're copying music.

Combine Clips

1 Record or import a series of audio clips and files. (Imported files can be in any format supported by Movie Maker.)

4 Click Save Movie, set the playback quality in the Save Movie dialog box, click OK, and then use the Save As dialog box to save the combined audio clip. If you want to save the project for future editing, click the Save Project button, and use the Save Project dialog box to save the project.

2 Click the Timeline button if the timeline isn't already displayed.

3 Drag the audio clips onto the timeline one at a time and in the order in which you want them to be played.

TRY THIS: Create and insert several audio clips. Click a clip, and drag the Start Trim or End Trim indicator on the timeline to crop the clips. Drag the left border of the clip onto the clip at its left to create a transition. Click the beginning of the timeline, and click the Play button to preview the audio track.

SEE ALSO: For information about cropping clips and using transitions between clips, see "Editing Your Movie" on page 90.

For information about recording WAV-type sound files, see "Creating a Sound File" on page 107.

Associating a Sound with an Event

If you want to hear audio cues for events in Windows XP—the closing of a program or the arrival of new mail, for example—you can assign sounds to these events. Windows XP comes with a variety of predesigned sound schemes that you can use, or you can create your own customized audio cues.

TIP: Put any WAV audio files that you want to use for events into the Media folder (you'll find it in the Windows folder), and the files will appear in the Sounds list, so you won't need to use the Browse button to locate them.

Use an Existing Sound Scheme

1 Open the Control Panel, click the Sounds, Speech, And Audio Devices category, and then click the Change The Sound Scheme task to display the Sounds And Audio Devices Properties dialog box.

2 On the Sounds tab, click a sound scheme in the list.

3 Click any event that's marked with a sound icon.

4 Click the Play Sound button to preview the sound scheme.

5 If you like the sound scheme, click OK.

TIP: You might or might not have numerous sound schemes available, depending on what other software you've installed, whether the computer was upgraded from a previous version of Windows, or whether someone else has created sound schemes. If you have only the one default Windows scheme, why not create a sound scheme of your own?

Create a Sound Scheme

1 If the Sounds And Audio Devices Properties dialog box isn't displayed, open it from the Control Panel.

2 On the Sounds tab, click an event to which you want to assign a sound.

3 Click a sound in the Sounds list, or use the Browse button to find a sound in another folder. Click None in the Sounds list to remove a sound from an event.

4 Use the Play Sound button to preview the sound. Continue to select events and assign the sounds you want.

5 Click Apply.

6 Click Save As, enter a name for the sound scheme you've created, and click OK.

7 Click OK.

8 Printing and Faxing

✳ NEW FEATURE

If, as many people do, you feel a bit daunted by the printing process because of previous unpleasant experiences with uncooperative printers, the first part of this section of the book will guide you painlessly through the printing maze.

If you have more than one printer, we'll show you how to designate one printer as your *default* printer, and how to *target* another printer when you don't want to—or can't—use the default printer. We'll also show you how to check the progress of your print jobs in the print queue. We know you'll welcome a great new feature in Microsoft Windows XP—a wizard that makes it really easy to print your photographs. With just a few clicks, you can choose the sizes, the number of copies, and the orientation you want for your pictures, and then you can just sit back and let Windows do the work. And if you've ever printed a Web page and been unhappily surprised by the chaotic result, you'll appreciate the ability Microsoft Internet Explorer gives you to easily print readable Web pages.

The second part of this section of the book is all about faxes and faxing. Provided you have a fax modem, you can use Fax Service to send and receive faxes using your computer rather than a separate fax machine. You can set up your computer to receive faxes automatically, or—if you have a single phone line that you use for both fax and voice—you can specify which calls you want to receive as faxes and which you want to answer yourself. And you can either set up your computer to automatically print incoming faxes, or you can help save the environment by reading your faxes on line.

Printing from a Program

In most programs, you can print a document on any printer that's installed on a computer or shared over a network. By using the Print dialog box, you can specify which printer to use and can customize the way your document is printed.

✅ **SEE ALSO:** For information about setting a printer as the default printer, see "Specifying a Default Printer" on page 114.

Print a Document

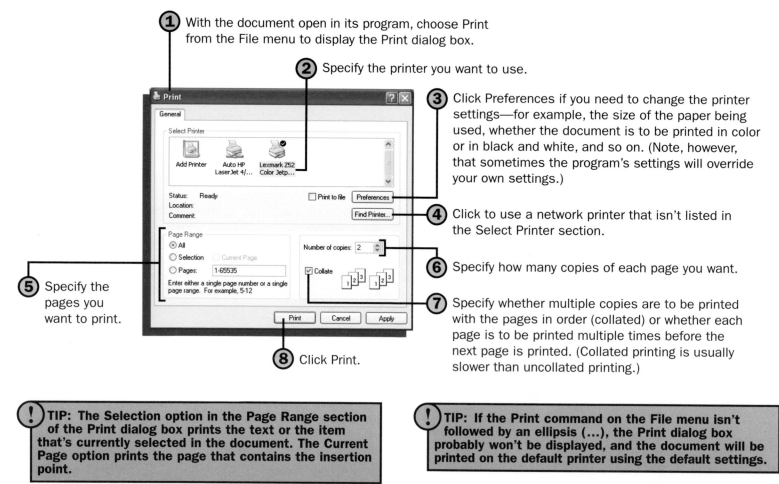

1. With the document open in its program, choose Print from the File menu to display the Print dialog box.

2. Specify the printer you want to use.

3. Click Preferences if you need to change the printer settings—for example, the size of the paper being used, whether the document is to be printed in color or in black and white, and so on. (Note, however, that sometimes the program's settings will override your own settings.)

4. Click to use a network printer that isn't listed in the Select Printer section.

5. Specify the pages you want to print.

6. Specify how many copies of each page you want.

7. Specify whether multiple copies are to be printed with the pages in order (collated) or whether each page is to be printed multiple times before the next page is printed. (Collated printing is usually slower than uncollated printing.)

8. Click Print.

! **TIP:** The Selection option in the Page Range section of the Print dialog box prints the text or the item that's currently selected in the document. The Current Page option prints the page that contains the insertion point.

! **TIP:** If the Print command on the File menu isn't followed by an ellipsis (...), the Print dialog box probably won't be displayed, and the document will be printed on the default printer using the default settings.

Printing a Document

When you want to print a document or a group of documents, you can print directly from Windows XP without having to start the program in which the document was created; that program, however, must be installed on your computer. It's a great convenience to be able to quickly send several documents to your printer and then walk away while Windows XP does all the work.

Print a Document Using the Default Printer

① Open the folder that contains the items you want to print, and select the document or documents.

② Right-click a selected document, and choose Print from the shortcut menu.

> **TIP:** Some programs require the use of the system default printer. To print documents that were created in any of those programs, you'll either have to use the default printer or have Windows XP switch the default-printer designation to the printer you want to use.

> **SEE ALSO:** For information about designating a printer as the default printer, see "Specifying a Default Printer" on page 114.

Print a Document Using a Specific Printer

① Choose Control Panel from the Start menu, click the Printers And Other Hardware category, and then click the View Installed Printers Or Fax Printers task to open the Printers And Faxes folder.

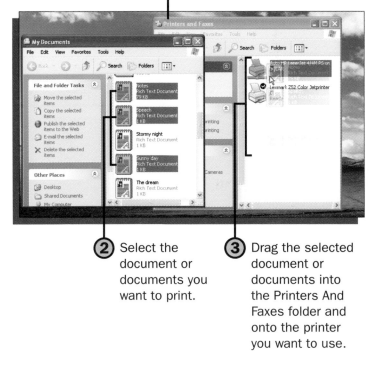

② Select the document or documents you want to print.

③ Drag the selected document or documents into the Printers And Faxes folder and onto the printer you want to use.

Specifying a Default Printer

Some programs are set up to print only on the system default printer. Other programs are set up to print on the system default printer but allow you to target, or change to, a different printer. If several printers are available, you can designate any one of them as your default printer.

Change the Default

1 Choose Control Panel from the Start menu, click the Printers And Other Hardware category, and then click the View Installed Printers Or Fax Printers task to open the Printers And Faxes folder.

2 Right-click the printer you want to use as the default printer.

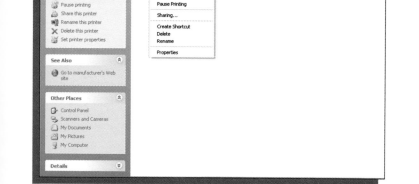

> **!** **TIP:** If there's a check mark next to the printer icon, the printer you've chosen has already been designated as the default printer.

> **✓** **SEE ALSO:** For information about printing on different printers, see "Printing from a Program" on page 112 and "Printing a Document" on page 113.

4 Close the Printers folder when you've finished.

3 Choose Set As Default Printer from the shortcut menu.

> **✋** **CAUTION:** If you have both a printer and Fax Service installed on your computer, make sure that the Fax printer isn't designated as your default printer. If it is, documents that you want to print might seem to have disappeared. (It's easy to accidentally set the Fax printer as the default when you delete an existing printer before you install a new one.)

Controlling Your Printing

When you send your documents to be printed, each print job is *queued*, or lined up, in the order in which it's received by the print server. You can see the progress of your print job in the queue, and you can temporarily suspend the printing of your document or even remove it from the queue if you want.

> **TIP:** Even after you've paused or canceled a print job, the printer might continue to print a page or two because those pages are already stored in the printer.

View the Queue

(1) Choose Control Panel from the Start menu, click the Printers And Other Hardware category, and then click the View Installed Printers Or Fax Printers task to open the Printers And Faxes folder.

(2) Double-click the printer you're using to open the print queue for that printer.

Documents in the print queue

(3) Note the names and details of the documents in the queue.

> **TIP:** To temporarily stop the printer from printing all the documents in the print queue, choose Pause Printing from the Printer menu. To cancel the printing of all the documents in the print queue, choose Cancel All Documents from the Printer menu.

Stop the Presses

(1) Right-click the name of your document.

(2) Choose the action you want from the shortcut menu:

- Pause to temporarily stop your document from printing

- Resume to resume printing after the document printing has been paused (note that Resume appears on the menu after you've chosen Pause)

- Restart to restart printing the document from the beginning after the document printing has been paused

- Cancel to delete the document from the print queue

Printing Your Photographs ⊕ NEW FEATURE

Printing your photographs used to be quite a challenge—depending on their format and resolution, your pictures might be printed in different sizes or in different orientations on the page. Windows XP now makes your life a lot easier by providing a wizard that lets you lay out the pictures just as you want them so that you get exactly the desired results every time.

Print the Pictures

1 Select the photograph you want to print. If you want to print multiple photos, make sure they're all in the same folder. However, you don't need to select them at this point.

2 Click Print This Picture to start the Photo Printing Wizard, and then click Next to enter the wizard.

5 Specify the layout you want.

8 Click Next to print the photos, and then click Finish to complete the wizard.

7 Look at the preview to make sure it's the way you want the pictures to be printed.

6 Specify the number of copies of each photo to be printed.

3 Select the check boxes for the photos you want to print and clear any check boxes that are already selected for the photos you don't want to print.

4 Click Next. On the Printing Options page of the wizard, specify the printer and printing preferences you want to use, and click Next again.

> **SEE ALSO:** For information about previewing your pictures, see "Viewing Pictures" on page 84.

Printing Web Pages

If you've ever visited a Web page whose content you found so interesting or informative that you wanted to print it out for yourself or for someone else to read, the printed result might have been less than satisfactory—odd-looking pages filled with cut-off text, for example, and an indecipherable hodgepodge of disconnected graphics, tables, frames, and text. However, using Internet Explorer, you can now convert Web pages into a printable form. All you need to do is specify how you want the pages to be set up, take a quick look at the layout to make sure it includes the items you want to print, and then print the pages.

Check the Layout

(1) With the Web page you want to print displayed in Internet Explorer, choose Print Preview from the File menu. Examine the page to make sure the layout is suitable for printing and that the information in the header and footer is what you want displayed.

(2) To print more than one page, click the Next Page button to see the additional page or pages.

Header and Footer Codes

Code	Result
&b *any text*	Right-aligns text.
&b *any text* &b	Centers text.
&d or &D	Inserts short date or long date.
&p	Inserts page number.
&P	Inserts total number of pages.
&t or &T	Inserts time in 12-hour or 24-hour format.
&u	Inserts Web page address.
&w	Inserts window title.

(3) If there's any truncated text, or if you want to change what's displayed in the header or footer, choose Page Setup from the File menu to display the Page Setup dialog box.

(4) Specify the paper size and the source of the paper—that is, which printer tray it's in.

(5) To change the contents of the header or footer, use the codes in the table on this page.

(7) Specify different margins if necessary.

(8) Click OK.

(9) Examine the layout based on your changes, and then click Print to print the Web pages.

(6) Specify whether you want the page to be printed in portrait (longer than wide) or landscape (wider than long) orientation.

Sending a Fax

With Fax Service installed, you can send a fax directly from your computer, whether it's a single-page fax with notes or a fax with several pages. To send only a few quick notes, simply enter them on a cover page. If you're sending a multiple-page document, you can decide whether or not to include a cover page.

SEE ALSO: For information about reviewing faxes you've sent and faxes that you've scheduled for later transmission, see "Reviewing a Fax You've Received" on page 121.

For information about setting up your fax, see "Setting Up for Faxing" on page 172.

Fax a Single-Page Note

1 Click the Start button, point your way through All Programs, Accessories, Communications, and Fax, and choose Send A Fax from the submenu. Click Next in the Send Fax Wizard to start the wizard.

2 Specify the recipient by either typing his or her name and fax number or clicking a name in the Address Book.

3 To specify a different country or to include an area code, select this check box.

4 If you typed the recipient's information, click the Add button to add that person to the list of recipients. Repeat the process to add other recipients.

5 Click Next when you've finished.

6 Specify a cover-page template, and enter the subject and any text you want on the cover page.

7 Click Next when you've finished.

8 Specify when you want the fax to be sent, and click Next. Preview the fax if you want, and then click Finish to send the fax to the fax queue.

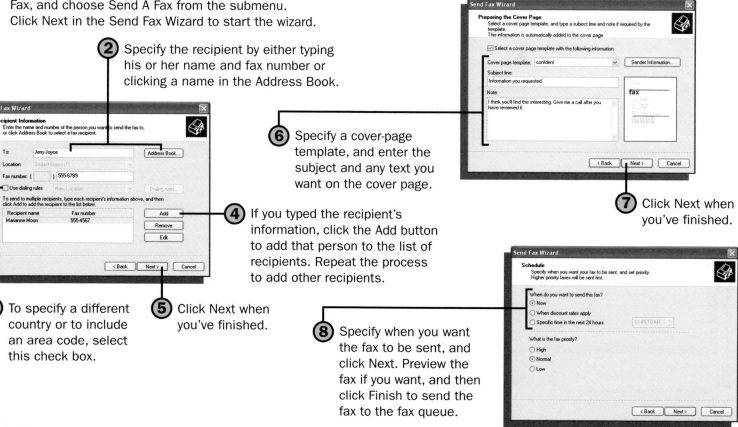

Fax a Document

(1) Open or create the document in its program.

(2) Choose Print from the File menu to display the Print dialog box.

CAUTION: If the program you're using doesn't display a Print dialog box, designate the Fax printer as the default printer before you choose the Print command.

SEE ALSO: For information about setting a default printer, see "Specifying a Default Printer" on page 114.

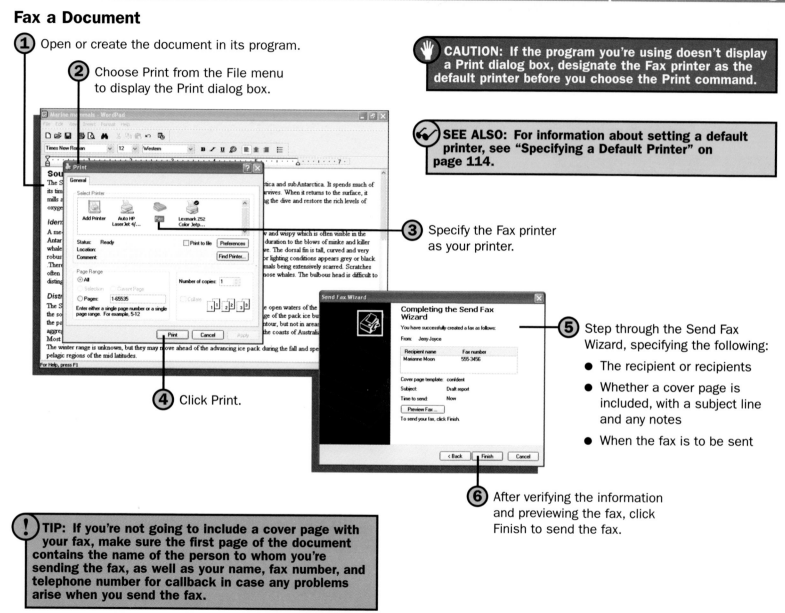

(3) Specify the Fax printer as your printer.

(4) Click Print.

(5) Step through the Send Fax Wizard, specifying the following:

- The recipient or recipients
- Whether a cover page is included, with a subject line and any notes
- When the fax is to be sent

(6) After verifying the information and previewing the fax, click Finish to send the fax.

TIP: If you're not going to include a cover page with your fax, make sure the first page of the document contains the name of the person to whom you're sending the fax, as well as your name, fax number, and telephone number for callback in case any problems arise when you send the fax.

Receiving a Fax

If you have a phone line dedicated to your computer and you set it to automatically receive faxes, all you have to do is review your received faxes. However, if you use your phone line for both voice and fax calls, you'll probably have your computer set up to receive faxes only when you tell it to do so.

SEE ALSO: For information about setting your computer to receive faxes either manually or automatically, see "Setting Up for Faxing" on page 172.

Receive a Fax Manually

1 When you receive the phone call and the notification that the line is ringing, click to receive the call.

2 In the Fax Monitor dialog box that appears, click the More button to see the details of the call. (After you've used the More button, it changes into the Less button.)

4 Click Hide after you've received the fax if you don't want the Fax Monitor dialog box on your Desktop.

3 If there's any problem with the fax, or if it's a junk fax and you want to terminate the fax reception before you've received the entire fax, click Disconnect.

Reviewing a Fax You've Received

After you receive a fax, you might want to review it, print it, save it, or send it to someone else. To review a fax, you use the Fax Console. You can also use the Fax Console to review faxes that you've sent, faxes that have yet to be sent, or a fax that you're currently receiving.

 TIP: You can also open the Fax Console by choosing Fax Console from the Fax submenu of the Start menu.

Read a Fax

(2) Click Inbox if it isn't already selected.

(4) Click a fax to select it, and then click the appropriate button:

● View to see the fax on the screen

● Print to send the fax to your printer

● Save As to save the fax to a folder as a TIF-format fax

● Mail To to include the fax as an attachment in an e-mail message

(1) Click the New Fax Received icon.

Print button — View button

Save As button — Mail To button

(5) Click Incoming to review the status of a fax that's currently being received.

(6) Click Outbox to review any faxes scheduled to be sent at a later time. To suspend or cancel the transmission of a fax, click the fax, and then click either the Pause button or the Delete button.

(3) Review the details of the received faxes.

(7) Click Sent Items to see the faxes you've sent. Click a fax in the list, and use the appropriate button to view, print, save, or e-mail the fax.

Viewing and Annotating a Fax

Save a tree—read your faxes on line! To do so, use the Windows Picture And Fax Viewer to read the fax, and even to annotate it with your comments, doodles, or whatever else you want to add.

View a Fax

① If the Fax Console isn't already open, display it by choosing Fax Console from the Fax submenu of the Start menu.

② Double-click the fax to be viewed.

! TIP: If you have a mouse with a wheel, rotating the wheel when you're using the Windows Picture And Fax Viewer changes the magnification of the image instead of scrolling the page as it does in many other programs.

③ Use the buttons In the Windows Picture And Fax Viewer to view the fax.

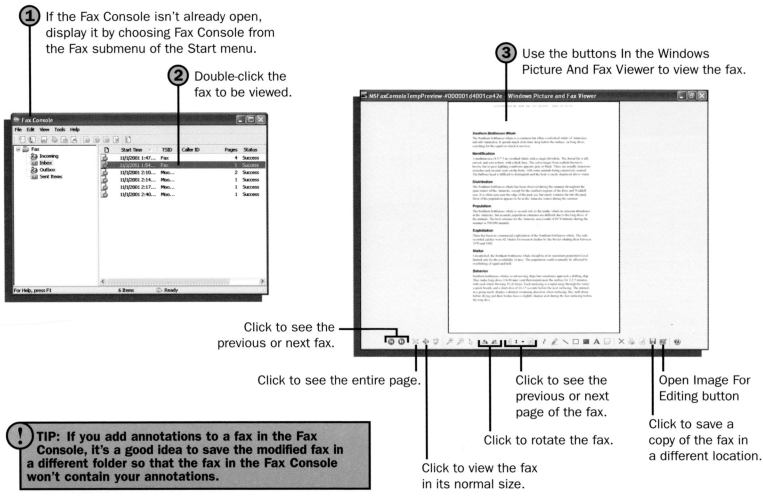

Click to see the previous or next fax.

Click to see the entire page.

Click to see the previous or next page of the fax.

Open Image For Editing button

Click to save a copy of the fax in a different location.

Click to rotate the fax.

Click to view the fax in its normal size.

! TIP: If you add annotations to a fax in the Fax Console, it's a good idea to save the modified fax in a different folder so that the fax in the Fax Console won't contain your annotations.

Annotate the Fax

(1) Use the appropriate annotation tool to mark up the fax:

- Freehand to draw a line in any shape
- Highlight to create a rectangular highlight
- Straight Line to draw a straight line
- Frame to draw a rectangular border around an area
- Solid Rectangle to draw a filled rectangle that obscures anything under it
- Attached Note to create a text box in which to enter a comment

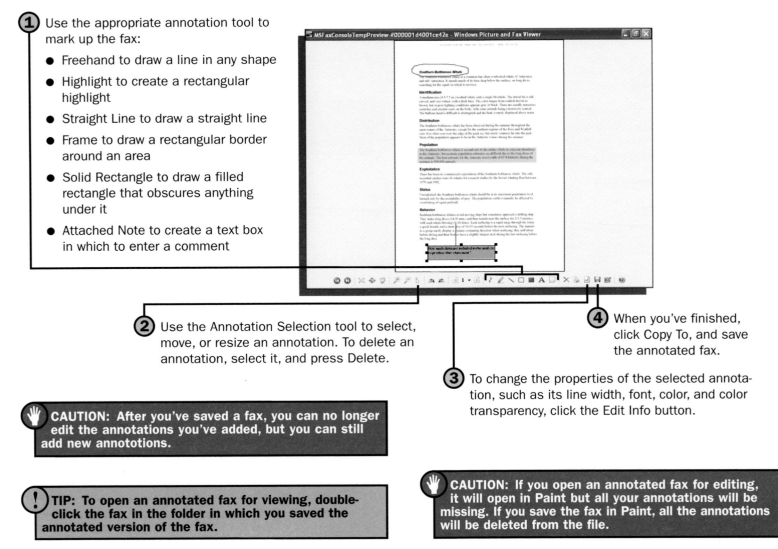

(2) Use the Annotation Selection tool to select, move, or resize an annotation. To delete an annotation, select it, and press Delete.

(4) When you've finished, click Copy To, and save the annotated fax.

(3) To change the properties of the selected annotation, such as its line width, font, color, and color transparency, click the Edit Info button.

CAUTION: After you've saved a fax, you can no longer edit the annotations you've added, but you can still add new annototions.

TIP: To open an annotated fax for viewing, double-click the fax in the folder in which you saved the annotated version of the fax.

CAUTION: If you open an annotated fax for editing, it will open in Paint but all your annotations will be missing. If you save the fax in Paint, all the annotations will be deleted from the file.

Creating a Fax Cover Page

Whenever you send a fax, it's good practice to include a cover page that contains information about the recipient and the sender, as well as the number of pages being sent. You can use the standard cover pages that Fax Service provides, or you can create your own cover page that contains the information you want in the design of your choice. The easiest way to create your own cover page is to start with one of the existing cover pages that Fax Service supplies, and then modify the page to your own use.

Create a Cover Page

1 If the Fax Console isn't already open, choose Fax Console from the Fax submenu of the Start menu. Choose Personal Cover Pages from the Tools menu to open the Personal Cover Pages dialog box.

! TIP: To modify an existing personal cover page, select it in the Personal Cover Pages dialog box, and click Open.

2 Click Copy, select the cover page you want to use as the basis for your own cover page, and click Open.

3 Click the cover page to select it, click Rename, type a name for your new cover page, and press Enter.

8 Save the cover page when you've finished, close the Fax Cover Page Editor, and then close the Personal Cover Pages dialog box.

Text tool   Drawing tools   Alignment tools

4 With the cover page selected, click Open.

Selection tool

5 For items that will be the same in all your faxes, use the Selection tool to select items, press Delete to remove unnecessary elements, and use the Text tool to insert text boxes and add formatted text.

6 For data that changes (supplied by the Sender Information or supplied by you when you complete the Send Fax Wizard), use the Insert menu to add data fields that insert information about the recipient, the sender, or the message.

7 Use the Selection tool to select multiple items, and then use the Alignment tools to arrange the elements.

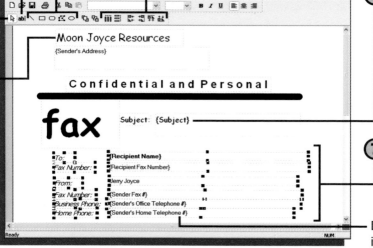

Data fields are replaced with information you've supplied.

Managing Files and Folders

We all know that to work productively, with minimal stress and frustration, we must *get organized!* That's where Microsoft Windows XP comes in. It supplies the framework—a basic file structure of drives and some ready-made folders, which you can use as is if it works for you. If not, you can create your own file- and folder-management system. Organize the files within the folders—alphabetically or by size, type, date, and so on. Move, copy, and rename files or groups of files. If you delete a file or folder by mistake, you can easily recover it. If you want the people who share the computer with you to have access to certain files and folders, you can put those items in folders that are designed to be shared. You can change the appearance of the windows in which you view your documents and folders, and, depending on the information you need, you can view them in any of six different views.

The Desktop is the place to put the files, folders, and other items you use every day, just as you do on a real desktop. To have immediate access to a report you're preparing or a performance review you're struggling with, put either the document itself or a shortcut to it on the Desktop.

You can transfer files or back up crucial information by copying the material onto removable disks—floppy disks or ZIP-type disks, for example. If you have a CD recorder installed on your computer, you can put the material on CDs—the CD Writing Wizard walks you helpfully through the process. Finally, we'll talk about the toolbars, which you use to navigate your way through the information on your computer, your intranet if you have one, and the Internet.

Organizing Your Files ⊕ NEW FEATURE

If you have a limited number of files, you can easily keep them all in a single folder, such as the My Documents folder. However, if you have many files, or files dealing with different projects, you'll probably want to organize them by placing them in individual folders. If a file doesn't have a suitably descriptive name, you can change it to one that's more useful, and if there's a group of related files, you can rename each file in the group with the same group name followed by consecutive numbering—for example, *stories*, *stories(1)*, *stories(2)*, and so on.

Move or Copy a File

1 Open the window containing the file or files you want to move or copy.

2 Select the file or files to be moved or copied.

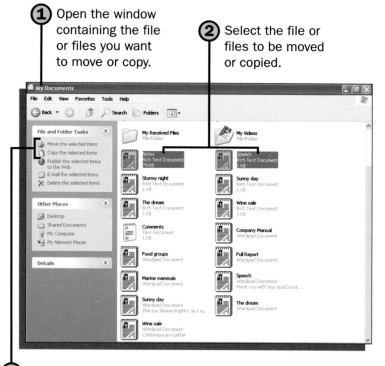

3 Click Move The Selected Items or Copy The Selected Items (or Move This File or Copy This File if you've selected only one file).

NEW FEATURE: In previous versions of Windows, you moved or copied files either by dragging them into a different window, or by using the Folders button in a folder window to show all the folders on the computer or in a network location and then dragging the files into one of those folders. You can still use either of these methods to move or copy files, but it's much easier to click the Move or Copy task.

TIP: To select a series of adjacent files, click the first file, hold down the Shift key, and click the last file in the group. To select nonadjacent files, hold down the Ctrl key as you click each file to be selected.

4 In the Move Items or the Copy Items dialog box, expand the listing by clicking plus signs until the destination folder is displayed. Click the destination folder.

5 If you want to create a new folder for the file or files, click Make New Folder.

6 Click Move or Copy to move or copy the file or files.

TIP: If you've created a new folder, Windows XP gives it the generic name New Folder in the Move Items or Copy Items dialog box. You'll want to rename the folder, using the same technique you use to rename a file.

Rename a File

① Click the file to select it.

② Click Rename This File.

③ With the file name selected, type a new name, or click to position the insertion point, and then edit the name. Press Enter when the name is correct.

> ✋ **CAUTION:** File names (or folder names) can be as long as 255 characters, but, because a long name is often truncated by a program, a descriptive short name is a better choice. You can use spaces and underscores in names, but you can't use the * : < > | ? " \ or / characters. If there's a file extension (up to three characters following the period at the end of the file name), don't change or delete it. Windows XP uses that extension to identify the type of file.

> ⚠ **TIP:** To delete a file or a group of files, select the file or group of files, and press the Delete key.

Rename a Group of Files

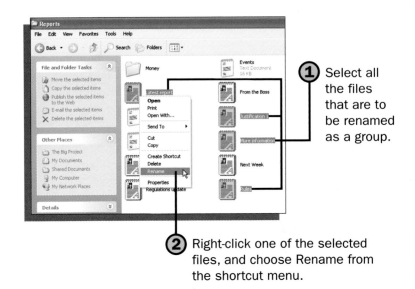

① Select all the files that are to be renamed as a group.

② Right-click one of the selected files, and choose Rename from the shortcut menu.

③ Type a name for the group, and then press Enter to rename the whole group.

Recovering a Deleted Item

If you accidentally delete a file, folder, or shortcut from your computer's hard disk, you can quickly recover the item either by undoing your action immediately or by restoring the deleted item from the Recycle Bin. The Recycle Bin holds all the files you've deleted from your hard disk(s) until you empty the bin or until it gets so full that the oldest files are deleted automatically.

> **! TIP:** When you've deleted a folder, you have to restore the entire folder. You can't open a deleted folder in the Recycle Bin and restore selected files.

Undo a Deletion

(1) Point to a blank spot on the Desktop or to a blank part of any folder window, and right-click.

(2) Choose Undo Delete from the shortcut menu.

The command is available only if the deletion was your most recent action.

Restore an Item

(1) Double-click the Recycle Bin icon on the Desktop to open the Recycle Bin window.

(2) Select the item or items to be recovered, and right-click.

(3) Click Restore This Item in the Recycle Bin Tasks list.

> **! TIP:** Windows XP remembers as many as three of your most recent actions, so if you executed an action after you deleted something, undo the action first, and then undo the deletion.

> **✋ CAUTION:** You can't recover any files that you've deleted from a removable disk, so be careful! Once they're gone, they're gone forever.

Changing the Window View

You can change the appearance of the windows that contain your files and folders so that the information is presented in the way that's the most useful for you.

Choose a View

1 In the window whose view you want to change, click the Views button.

2 Click the view you want to use.

> **SEE ALSO:** For information about the different views, see "Windows Views" on page 130.

Arrange the Information

1 Point to Arrange Icons By on the View menu, and choose the type of item by which you want to sort the listing.

2 Point to Arrange Icons By on the View menu again, and choose one of the following options from the submenu:

- Show In Groups to group items (folders, files, and so on) under classifications based on the item by which the list is sorted

- Auto Arrange to have icons automatically repositioned to fill any gaps in the arrangement

- Align To Grid to have icons snap to an invisible grid so that they line up with each other even though the alignment might leave gaps in the arrangement

3 If you want to use an additional option, point to Arrange Icons By again, and choose the additional option. (Note that not all options are available for all views.)

Windows Views

Windows XP can display the contents of a folder window in one of six available views, and you can modify each view in several ways. You can choose the view you want from the View menu, or you can click the Views button on the Standard Buttons toolbar. Then you use the View menu to change the way the items are arranged. You'll probably want to experiment to see which view is best suited for your work and for the contents of the folder. For example, you might want to use Icons view in a folder that contains only a few files of different types, Details view when you're looking for files that were created on a specific date, Thumbnails view when you're managing pictures, and Filmstrip view when you're reviewing the pictures.

The six views are described on these two pages.

Filmstrip: Displays a large preview of the selected picture file, together with thumbnail views of all the files and subfolders in the folder. This view is available only for folders that have been set up for pictures.

Thumbnails: Displays a miniature representation of the file or folder. If the file is a picture, the picture is displayed. If you've saved a preview of the file, the preview is usually displayed. For a folder that has been customized to use an identifying picture, or for a folder that contains multiple pictures, the identifying picture or the first few pictures contained in the folder are displayed. If no picture or preview is available for the file or folder, an icon is displayed.

Tiles: Displays large icons with information about the file next to each icon. The information that's displayed changes depending on which property (date or size, for example) you've used to arrange the icons.

Filmstrip view   Thumbnails view   Tiles view

Icons: Displays icons that indicate whether each item represented is a folder or a file. The name of the item is listed below the icon.

List: Displays small icons representing folders and files in a vertical listing that can snake through multiple columns. The name of the item is listed next to the icon. Note that in List view you can't arrange the items in groups.

Details: Displays small icons in a single-column list that shows the name of the item and includes details such as size, type, and date.

Once you've chosen the view you want, Windows XP offers more options. In each view, you can arrange the way the files are sorted—for example, you can arrange them in order by name, size, file type, or date. If you prefer, you can arrange the files in groups, based on the way they were sorted—for example, if you've sorted the files by size, you can then group them according to their relative sizes in subgroups of tiny, small, medium, or large files. In all views, you choose the arrangement you want from the View menu. In Details view, you can also click the title of a column to sort by that column.

Windows XP doesn't stop there, of course. You can change the look of each icon in the folder, or add a picture to the folder itself. By defining the types of files that will be stored in a folder, you can customize the way the folder is set up and what tools you'll have available. You'll find more information about customizing folders in "Customizing Your Folders" on page 188.

Icons view

List view

Details view

Compressing Files

Compressed folders are special folders that use compression software to decrease the sizes of the files they contain. Compressed folders are useful for reducing the file size of standard documents and programs, but they're invaluable when you're storing large graphics files such as bitmaps or when you're transferring large files by e-mail.

Create a Compressed Folder

SEE ALSO: For information about encrypting compressed folders for increased security, see "Protecting Your Files with a Password" on page 201.

For more information about compressing an entire drive, or compressing an existing folder using the NTFS file system, see "Compressing a Drive or a Folder" on page 213.

1 Select the file or files to be copied to a compressed folder.

2 Right-click one of the selected files, point to Send To on the shortcut menu, and choose Compressed (Zipped) Folder from the submenu. Rename the compressed folder if necessary.

Zippered-folder icon denotes a compressed folder.

3 Drag any other files onto the compressed folder icon to copy those files to the compressed folder.

TIP: A compressed folder is compatible with file-compression programs that support the ZIP file format.

Use a Compressed File

① Double-click the compressed folder to open it.

② Double-click an item in the folder to open it in its associated program. If the item is a program, double-click it to run it. (Note, though, that not all files and programs will function properly from the compressed folder.)

④ To decompress all the files in the folder and copy them to another folder, click Extract All Files.

⑤ Step through the Extraction Wizard, specifying where the files are to be extracted, or copied, to.

③ To decompress a single file, select it, click Copy This File, and specify which folder you want the file to be copied to.

TRY THIS: Compress a large file (or a group of files) by placing it in a compressed folder. Click the compressed-folder icon, and click E-Mail This File in the File And Folder Tasks list. Send the folder, which is now listed as a ZIP-type file, to the person who needs it. If the recipient's operating system isn't equipped with the compressed-folders feature, he or she will need to use a third-party compression program that uses ZIP-type compressed files to open the files.

CAUTION: Compressed folders preserve the contents of most files, but it's possible that you could lose some data when you're using certain file formats. It's wise to test your file format in a compressed folder before you move valuable files into that folder.

Adding Files and Folders to the Desktop

The Windows XP Desktop is more than just a place for pictures and icons. You can use the Desktop to store frequently used files and folders for quick access, or to store parts of files for later use.

Add a File

(1) Open the folder window that contains the file you want to put on the Desktop.

(3) From the shortcut menu that appears, choose either to copy or move the file onto the Desktop, or to create a shortcut to the document.

(2) Hold down the *right* mouse button and drag the document onto the Desktop.

> **SEE ALSO:** For information about accessing documents from a toolbar, see "Navigating with Toolbars" on page 144.
>
> For information about displaying or hiding the standard icons (such as My Computer) on the Desktop, see "Customizing the Desktop" on page 180.

Add a Folder

(1) Right-click a blank spot on the Desktop.

(2) Point to New on the shortcut menu, and choose Folder from the submenu.

(3) Type a name for the new folder, and press Enter.

> **TIP:** Items that you've placed on the Desktop are actually stored in the Documents And Settings folder under your name.

Save a File to the Desktop

1 Create a file in your program.

2 Choose Save from the File menu to display the Save As dialog box.

3 Click Desktop in the Save In drop-down list.

4 Type a name for the file.

5 Click Save.

Save Part of a File to the Desktop

1 Select the part of the file you want to save.

2 Drag the selection onto the Desktop. (You'll notice that Windows XP puts a "scrap" icon on the Desktop.)

> **!** **TIP:** If the program you're using doesn't support dragging and dropping, and you want to save a section of text as a scrap on the Desktop, copy the selected text, right-click a blank spot on the Desktop, and choose Paste from the shortcut menu.

> **TRY THIS:** Start WordPad, and type some text. Select the text and drag it onto the Desktop. Start a new document in WordPad, type some text, and then drag the WordPad scrap from the Desktop into the WordPad document.

> **!** **TIP:** Scraps can also be stored in folders, so you can organize them just as you can any other files.

Sharing Files with Other Users

Each user of your computer has his or her own set of folders in which to keep documents, music, and so on. If you want the other people who use your computer to have access to certain files, you can place those files in special folders that are designed specifically for sharing. If you're connected to a network, the files in these folders are also available to other people on the network.

! TIP: If you open a folder that doesn't show a Shared Documents item in the Other Places list, but you want to copy a file from the folder to the Shared Documents folder, click the Folders button on the Standard Buttons toolbar, and drag the file onto the Shared Documents folder shown in that list.

Share a File

(1) Open the folder that contains the file or files you want to share.

(2) Select the file. If you want to share several files, select all of them.

(3) Drag the file or files onto the Shared Documents item. Anyone who uses the computer can now access the file or files in the Shared Documents folder.

TRY THIS: Select a file, click the Copy This File task in the File And Folder Tasks list, select the Shared Documents folder in the Copy Items dialog box, and click Copy. The file has now been copied instead of moved.

SEE ALSO: For information about making your folders private so that other users of your computer can't access them, see "Keeping Your Files Private" on page 196.

Creating Quick Access to a File or Folder

If you use a particular file or folder frequently, you can access it quickly by placing a shortcut to it on the Desktop, on the Start menu, or just about anywhere you want. A shortcut to a document opens the document in its default program; a shortcut to a program file starts the program; a shortcut to a folder opens the folder in a window.

Create a Shortcut to a File or Folder

1 Open a window that contains the file or folder.

2 Right-click the file or folder, and choose Create Shortcut from the shortcut menu.

3 If you don't like the shortcut's name, with the shortcut still selected, click Rename This File, and type a new name for the shortcut. Press Enter when you've finished.

4 Drag the shortcut to a destination in the Other Places list, or click the Copy This File item in the File And Folder Tasks list to move the shortcut to the location you want.

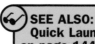 **SEE ALSO:** For information about displaying the Quick Launch toolbar, see "Navigating with Toolbars" on page 144.

For information about adding items to the Start menu, see "Customizing the Start Menu" on page 184.

Copying Files from and to a Removable Disk

A quick and easy way to transfer files is to put them on a floppy disk or some other type of removable disk. When you receive a removable disk, you can copy the files from it to your computer. When you want to give some files to a friend or coworker, you can copy the files onto a disk for that person. You can also use a removable disk to back up and save your critical files in case you accidentally delete a file from your computer, or to safeguard against losing files because of a power failure or some other problem with your computer.

Copy Files from a Disk

1 Insert the disk into the drive. If a window displaying the disk contents doesn't open, choose My Computer from the Start menu to display the My Computer window, and then double-click the drive to open a folder window for the drive.

2 Select a file (or a group of files).

3 Drag the selection to a destination in the Other Places list to copy the file or files to that destination. If the destination you want isn't listed, click Copy The Selected Items to copy the file to the destination you want.

Copy Files to a Disk

1 With the removable disk in its drive, locate and select the file or files you want to copy to the removable disk.

2 Right-click one of the selected files, point to Send To on the shortcut menu, and choose the removable disk from the submenu. Wait for all the selected files to be copied.

> ✋ **CAUTION: Although you manually eject a floppy disk by pushing the button next to the drive, you should remove most other types of removable disks by right-clicking the drive in the My Computer folder window, and then choosing Eject from the shortcut menu.**

Managing a Removable Disk

Removable disks are invaluable items, but they do require some management. When you want to copy several items onto a disk, you need to monitor how much space is available on the disk, especially if you use the small-capacity 3½-inch disks. If you frequently reuse your removable disks, you might also find it necessary to occasionally format a disk. (Formatting a disk removes all the files from the disk and resets the disk's filing system so that it's prepared for new content.)

Check the Amount of Space on a Disk

① With the disk in the drive, choose My Computer from the Start menu to display the My Computer folder window.

② Right-click the drive, and choose Properties from the shortcut menu to display the disk's Properties dialog box.

③ On the General tab of the Properties dialog box, note the amount of free space on the disk.

④ Click OK when you've finished.

Format a Disk

① If you're certain the disk doesn't contain any files that you'll need again, in the My Computer folder window, right-click the drive, and choose Format from the shortcut menu to display the Format dialog box.

② Select this check box to quickly remove the listings of files (but not the content of the files, which is overwritten by the new files) from the disk and to free up the entire disk for new files. Clear the check box to fully remove all the old files for added security or if you run into a problem with the current disk formatting— for example, if you can't format the disk using quick formatting.

③ Select this check box if you want to use a floppy disk to start up your computer and to run it using MS-DOS. (This option applies to floppy disks only.)

④ Click Start, and then click OK when you're warned about erasing all items on the disk. Wait for the disk to be formatted. Click OK when the formatting has been completed.

⑤ Click Close to close the Format dialog box.

✋ **CAUTION:** When you either format a floppy disk or delete files from it, the files are permanently deleted and can't be recovered from the Recycle Bin.

❗ **TIP:** To delete all the files on a removable disk, open the folder window for the disk drive, press Ctrl+A to select all the files, and then press Delete.

Copying Files to a CD ⊕ NEW FEATURE

If you have a CD recorder (sometimes called a CD burner) installed on your computer, you can copy your files to a CD for safe storage or easy distribution. To do so, you copy all the files you want to include on the CD into a temporary storage area, and then, after all the files are assembled, you copy them from the temporary storage area to the CD. You can continue copying files to the CD until it's full.

Gather and Copy Your Files and Folders

1 Using My Computer, My Documents, or any other folder window, locate and select the file or files and/or the folder or folders you want to copy.

2 Right-click one of the selected items, point to Send To on the shortcut menu, and choose CD Drive. Repeat for other files and folders from different locations to gather all the items you want to copy into one temporary storage area.

Organize the CD

1 In the My Computer folder window, double-click your CD drive to display the folder window for the drive.

2 Review the files that you've gathered to be copied to the CD.

3 If you want to organize some of the files by placing them in a folder, click Make A New Folder, name the folder, and then drag the files into the folder.

Create the CD

1 When you've assembled and organized all the files, click Write These Files To CD in the CD Writing Tasks list to start the CD Writing Wizard.

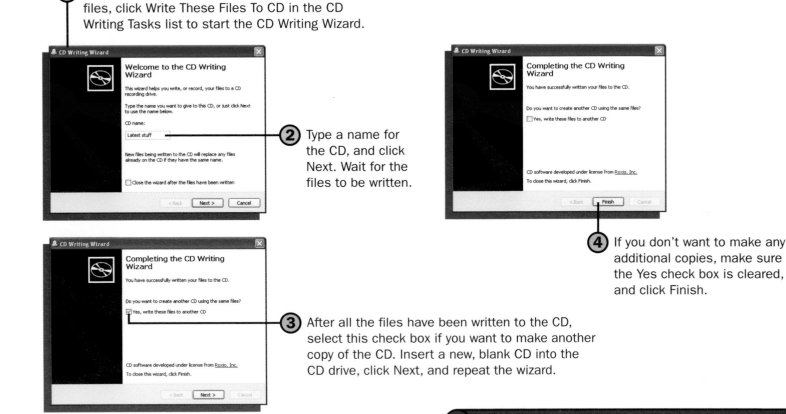

2 Type a name for the CD, and click Next. Wait for the files to be written.

4 If you don't want to make any additional copies, make sure the Yes check box is cleared, and click Finish.

3 After all the files have been written to the CD, select this check box if you want to make another copy of the CD. Insert a new, blank CD into the CD drive, click Next, and repeat the wizard.

TRY THIS: In the CD Drive window, press Ctrl+A to select everything. Right-click any of the selected items, and choose Properties from the shortcut menu. Note the number of files and folders, and especially the size of all the items on the disk. Click OK. The combined size of all the files should give you a good idea as to whether or not all your files will fit on the CD.

TIP: Microsoft Plus! For Windows XP includes a program for creating CD labels and covers for CD cases.

Finding a File

If you don't remember the exact name or location of a file, tell Windows XP what you do remember—for example, the document type, all or part of its name, when it was last modified, the drive or the computer where it resides—and then let Windows XP do the searching for you.

TIP: You can also search for a document by clicking the Search button in any folder window. Unless you change the search area, the search will be limited to the current folder and any subfolders it contains.

Find a File

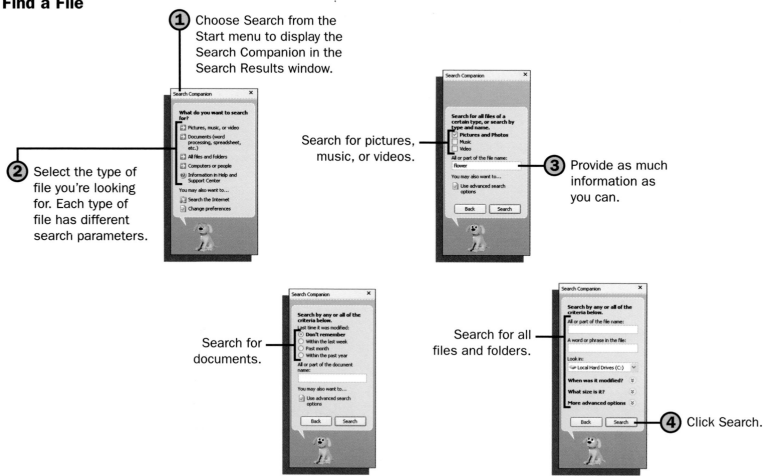

1 Choose Search from the Start menu to display the Search Companion in the Search Results window.

2 Select the type of file you're looking for. Each type of file has different search parameters.

Search for pictures, music, or videos.

3 Provide as much information as you can.

Search for documents.

Search for all files and folders.

4 Click Search.

Use the Results

① Review the results of the search.

② If there are too many files listed to easily find the file or folder you want, or if the file you want wasn't found, select one of the items to refine the search.

③ If the file you want is listed, right-click it, and choose the action you want from the shortcut menu.

> ⚠️ **TIP:** If you find yourself searching frequently, you can have Windows XP conduct a faster and more extensive search by using the Indexing Services. To enable the Indexing Services, instead of choosing the type of file in the Search Companion area, click **Change Preferences**, and then click **With Indexing Services**. The Indexing Services feature speeds up a search but, because it frequently needs to update the index of all your files whenever you make changes to the contents of the hard disk, it might slow down your computer's normal operating speed.

> ⚠️ **TIP:** If you're not sure whether a file is the one you want, point to the file, and read the information in the pop-up description that appears. If you want more information, right-click the file, and choose Properties from the shortcut menu.

Navigating with Toolbars

There are four toolbars associated with the Windows XP taskbar, and they provide access to programs, folders, and documents as well as to Internet and intranet sites.

Display a Toolbar

 Right-click a blank spot on the taskbar.

2 Point to Toolbars on the shortcut menu, and choose the toolbar you want to display. (A toolbar with a check mark next to its name is one that's already displayed.)

3 Double-click the toolbar if it isn't already expanded.

4 If the toolbar doesn't expand, right-click a blank spot on the taskbar, choose Lock The Taskbar from the shortcut menu, and repeat step 3.

> **SEE ALSO:** For information about creating your own toolbars and modifying the toolbars in folder windows, see "Displaying and Arranging the Toolbars" on page 183.

> **TRY THIS:** Right-click a blank spot on the taskbar, and choose Toolbars from the shortcut menu to display several toolbars. Double-click the small vertical bar on a toolbar to maximize the toolbar's length. Double-click the vertical bar again to restore the toolbar's original size. Drag the vertical bar to create a custom-size toolbar.

The Taskbar's Toolbars

Toolbar	Function
Address	Opens the item when you specify its address. The address can be the path and the file or folder name, a program name, a computer on the network, or even the Internet address of a Web page.
Links	Links you to the same locations that are shown on the Internet Explorer Links toolbar.
Desktop	Provides quick access to the icons, files, folders, and shortcuts on the Desktop.
Quick Launch	Launches Internet Explorer, Outlook Express, and Windows Media Player, or minimizes all the windows on the Desktop.

See All the Buttons

1 If an entire toolbar or taskbar isn't displayed, double-click the small vertical bar on the toolbar.

2 If any of the buttons on a toolbar are still not visible, click the right-facing chevrons to display the hidden items.

3 If all the buttons on the taskbar are still not visible, use the up or down arrow to scroll through all the items.

10 Networking

NEW FEATURE

NEW FEATURE

Networking—once a requirement only in large corporations—is now almost a necessity in a multi-computer household, a home office, or a small business. With two or more computers connected, you can access files and folders on other computers that have been set up for sharing, and you can share the files and folders on your computer with other people. (And, of course, if there are items to which you want to limit other people's access—your private files, for example—you can do so.) But that's not all—a network also enables you to share printers, to share an Internet connection, and to communicate over the network using Windows Messenger (see "Sending Instant Messages" on page 68) or, alternatively, NetMeeting, which we'll discuss in this section. One of the nice things about NetMeeting is that you don't have to be connected to the Internet to have a conversation or a quick meeting with a friend or coworker.

Windows XP also makes it easy for you to telecommute—the Remote Desktop Connection allows you to sit at your home computer and actually work on the Desktop of your office computer, provided your office computer is running Windows XP Professional or Windows XP Server. It's a great way to get some of your work done from the comfort of your home. If you need to gain access to your office network from your home computer, you can do so via a remote connection: by dialing up a network server, for example, or using the Internet to create a VPN (Virtual Private Network), which ensures a secure connection to another computer.

Exploring Your Network

Windows XP automatically searches for the shared folders, printers, and whatever other items are shared on your network's computers. You can also open a window to all the shared folders on a specific computer, or you can connect to a computer that's in a different workgroup.

SEE ALSO: For information about setting up your network, see "Setting Up a Network" on page 174.

Connect to a Shared Folder

① Choose My Network Places from the Start menu to open the My Network Places window.

② Double-click a shared folder to access its contents.

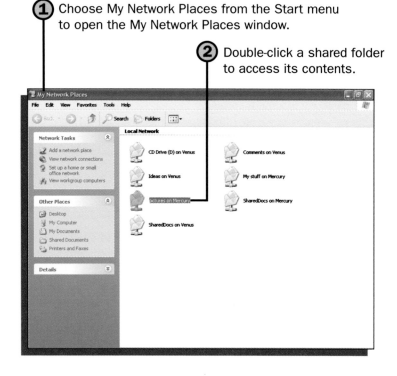

Connect to a Computer

① In the My Network Places window, click View Workgroup Computers.

② Double-click the computer whose shared folders and resources you want to view or access.

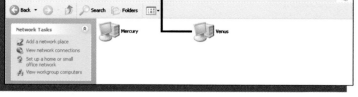

TIP: If you've set up your network but you don't see My Network Places on the Start menu, choose My Computer from the Start menu, and click My Network Places in the Other Places list. Close the window. My Network Places should now be listed on the Start menu.

Connect to a Computer in a Different Workgroup

1 In the My Network Places window, click Add A Network Place, and then click Next to start the Add Network Place Wizard.

! **TIP: To see the folders and other resources that are being shared by your computer over the network, look at the list of workgroup computers, and then double-click your own computer's name in the list. Review the shared folders and their contents. Only shared items are displayed.**

2 Step through the wizard, specifying

● That you want to choose another network location.

● The address of the computer and the shared folder, in the form *computername**sharedfolder*.

● Whether you want to accept the proposed name for the connection or prefer to rename it.

TRY THIS: Once you've connected to a computer in a different workgroup, you'll have access to all the computers in that workgroup. To see those computers, click View Workgroup Computers in the My Network Places window, and then click the Up button on the Standard Buttons toolbar. Double-click the workgroup to see all the computers in the workgroup.

3 Connect to the shared folder as you'd connect to any shared folder from My Network Places. If you're asked for a user name and password, enter a valid user name and password for access to that computer, and click OK.

Sharing Items over the Network

Once you've set up your network, you can share all the documents that are stored in the Shared Documents folder. If this folder contains any subfolders, you can share their contents too. You can also designate which folders and printers on your computer you want to share with other network users.

Share a File

1 Use My Computer to locate the file you want to share.

2 Drag the file onto the Shared Documents item in the Other Places list.

> **⚠ TIP: The Shared Documents folder is shared by default over the entire network at the time networking is set up. If you want to share the files in the Shared Documents folder only with people who log on to your computer rather than with everyone on the network, right-click Shared Documents in My Computer, choose Sharing And Security, and, on the Sharing tab, clear the Share This Folder On The Network check box, and then click OK.**

Share a Folder

1 Use My Computer to open the drive or folder containing the folder you want to share.

2 Right-click the folder you want to share, and choose Sharing And Security from the shortcut menu to display the folder's Properties dialog box.

3 On the Sharing tab, select this check box.

4 Either accept the proposed name or type a new name for the shared folder.

6 Click OK.

5 If you're going to allow others to have full control of the folder—that is, to be able to add, delete, modify, and rename files in the folder—select this check box. To allow read-only access—that is, users of the network can see and open the files in the folders, but they can't save or modify any files—clear this check box.

Share a Printer

① Choose Control Panel from the Start menu, click the Printers And Other Hardware category, and click the View Installed Printers Or Fax Printers task. Right-click the printer to be shared, and choose Sharing from the shortcut menu to display the printer's Properties dialog box.

② On the Sharing tab, click the Share This Printer option.

③ Either accept the proposed name or type a new name for the shared printer.

⑤ Select the check boxes for the relevant operating systems.

⑥ Click OK.

④ If there are computers on your network that use an operating system other than Windows XP or Windows 2000, and if those computers will be using your printer, click Additional Drivers.

⑦ If prompted, insert the Windows XP CD into your computer's CD drive, and click OK. Wait for the drivers to be installed. Click OK in the Additional Drivers dialog box, and click OK in the printer's Properties dialog box.

! **TIP:** If you want to limit your shared printer's availability, click the Advanced tab of the printer's Properties dialog box, and set the times during which the printer will be available.

About Networks

A network, whether it's large or small, gives you the ability to connect computers so that they can communicate with each other. Windows XP Home Edition is designed for a small network (a *peer-to-peer network*), where all the computers communicate directly with each other. To work on a larger network (a *client-server network*), where communication between computers is routed through a server, you'll need to use Windows XP Professional. On a home network, one of your computers acts as a *server,* or *host,* on your peer-to-peer network. The host does two things: it assigns each computer on your network a unique identifying number (an IP address), and it coordinates traffic to the Internet through its shared Internet connection. Other than providing those services, the host computer is just like all the other computers on your network.

On a small network, the organizational unit is the workgroup. Members of the same workgroup can easily access shared files, printers, and other resources. In most cases, working on a home network will be easiest if all the computers are members of the same workgroup. Even if you have separate workgroups, however, you can still access the same resources, although it might take a little bit of extra work the first time you try it. Windows XP has a special tool called a *netcrawler* that inspects the network and finds all the shared resources. If you have different workgroups, the list of shared resources on the other workgroups might not always be current.

Computers can be connected to a network in a variety of ways: by direct connections with cables, with wires that go through network hubs, with connections through your power or phone lines, or even without any wires at all. With so many options, setting up a network can be a simple job or a truly miserable experience. Some connections use "standard" network software and settings; others require special software and configurations. If you're installing a network from a network installation kit, the kit should include all the instructions and software you'll need to get the network set up. If you're simply installing a network card in each computer, and Windows XP doesn't detect and set up each newly installed network card, use the setup CD or disk to install each card. If you don't have a setup program, run the Add New Hardware Wizard from the Control Panel. For more information, see "Adding Hardware" on page 176.

Windows XP also has a special tool for dealing with different types of network configurations on a single network. If, for example, you have one computer that has a wireless network connection to a couple of computers and also has a network connection using cables to a couple more computers, Windows XP can connect these two networks by installing a *bridge* on the first computer to provide a connection to both networks.

When Windows XP is installed, network software (called the *TCP/IP protocol*) is installed too. This software enables you to communicate over the Internet and on your own network. With standard network configurations, and on special networks where the software drivers are already installed, Windows XP is almost ready to run. Before you use the network, though, you'll need to run the Network Setup Wizard to identify your computer to the network and to specify the types of access you want over the network. You'll also need to specify whether you want to share your Internet connection or any of your files. If you're creating a new network, you'll need to run the wizard on each computer so that the proper settings and software are installed on each machine. Once the network is set up, you'll find that sharing resources is easy and convenient.

Creating a Connection to a Network Folder

If you frequently use one particular folder on the network, you can access that folder quickly by assigning a drive letter to it. By doing so, you will not only gain quick access to the folder from My Computer but will also be able to access the folder in programs that don't let you browse My Network Places to find a file.

TRY THIS: Create a network drive. Open My Computer, and verify that the drive is listed in that window. Start a program, use the drive to open or save a file, and then close the program. Right-click My Computer, and choose Disconnect from the shortcut menu to delete the drive assignment.

Assign a Drive

1. Choose My Network Places from the Start menu.

2. Click View Workgroup Computers in the Network Tasks list.

3. Double-click the computer that contains the shared folder.

4. Right-click the folder, and choose Map Network Drive from the shortcut menu.

5. In the Map Network Drive dialog box, click a drive letter for this folder.

6. Clear this check box if you want to use the drive assignment during this session only, or keep the check box selected if you want to reestablish this drive assignment each time the computer is started.

7. Click Finish.

Controlling a Shared Dial-Up Internet Connection ⊛ NEW FEATURE

When a network is set up to share a dial-up connection to the Internet, the connection can be left open even when no one is using it. However, if you're concerned about tying up the phone line or if you want to economize on the phone or ISP connection charges, you can have the connection end automatically when no one is using it. Alternatively, you can manually end the connection from your computer even if the phone line isn't connected to your computer.

Configure the Connection

1 On the computer that's hosting the Internet connection, choose My Network Places from the Start menu, and click View Network Connections in the Network Tasks list. Click the Internet connection you use, and click Change Setting Of This Connection in the Network Tasks list to display the connection's Properties dialog box.

2 On the Options tab, set a short time for the computer to be idle before it hangs up the connection.

3 Click OK.

End the Connection

1 On the computer that's using the Internet connection over the network, choose My Network Places from the Start menu, and click View Network Connections in the Network Tasks list to display the Network Connections dialog box.

2 Click the Internet connection you're using to select it.

3 Click Disconnect This Connection.

> ✎ **TRY THIS: To set up your computer to quickly hang up the connection over the network, right-click the connection in the Network Connections window, and choose Properties from the shortcut menu. Select the Show Icon In Notification Area When Connected check box to show an icon in the notification area of the taskbar, and click OK. To disconnect, click the icon, and then click Disconnect in the Status dialog box that appears.**

Communicating over the Network

Windows Messenger is a great way to communicate over the Internet, but you can use it over your network only if you're connected to the Internet. Fortunately, there's a Windows XP feature called NetMeeting that provides similar functionality over your network without tying up—or being slowed down by—your connection to the Internet.

> **!** **TIP: NetMeeting has been replaced by Windows Messenger for most uses, but the tools in the two features are very similar. However, you can't use Windows Messenger without being connected to the Internet, and, because NetMeeting allows video from only one computer, you can't have a two-way video session in NetMeeting as you can in Windows Messenger.**

Start NetMeeting

① Choose Run from the Start menu to display the Run dialog box.

② Type **conf** and press Enter.

③ If you haven't used NetMeeting before, step though the NetMeeting Setup Wizard. Make sure that you choose not to connect to the Internet directory unless you're planning to use NetMeeting over the Internet as well as on your network.

Connect to a Computer

① With NetMeeting running on both computers, type the name of the computer you're calling, and press Enter. Wait for the other person to answer your call.

③ Click the End Call button when you've finished.

② Use the tools to conduct your conversation or meeting.

> **SEE ALSO: For information about using the Whiteboard, see "Illustrating Your Conversation" on page 72.**

Controlling a Computer on Your Network

Do you want to gain full access to one computer from another over your network? By sharing a computer's Desktop using NetMeeting, you can access and run programs, reorganize files, and so on—all from the other computer's Desktop.

> **SEE ALSO:** For information about using Desktop Sharing with a computer that's running Windows XP Professional, see "Controlling a Computer at Your Workplace" on page 156.

Share the Desktop

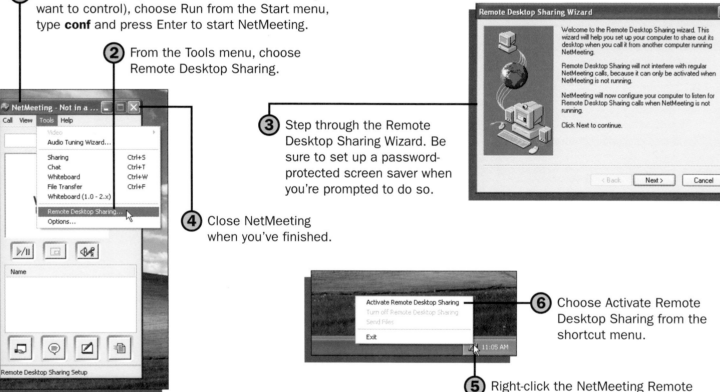

(1) On the other computer on the network (the one you want to control), choose Run from the Start menu, type **conf** and press Enter to start NetMeeting.

(2) From the Tools menu, choose Remote Desktop Sharing.

(3) Step through the Remote Desktop Sharing Wizard. Be sure to set up a password-protected screen saver when you're prompted to do so.

(4) Close NetMeeting when you've finished.

(6) Choose Activate Remote Desktop Sharing from the shortcut menu.

(5) Right-click the NetMeeting Remote Desktop Sharing icon in the notification area of the taskbar.

Connect to the Computer

1 On the computer that you'll be using to remotely control another computer, start NetMeeting, and click the Place Call button to display the Place A Call dialog box.

2 Enter the name of the computer you're calling.

3 Select this check box.

4 Click Call.

> **TIP:** Using a password-protected screen saver prevents other people from using your computer when it's unattended.

5 Enter your password when prompted, and click OK.

6 Work from the Desktop of the computer you're controlling remotely.

7 Click the End Call button in NetMeeting when you've finished.

> **TIP:** To temporarily deactivate Remote Desktop Sharing on your computer, right-click the NetMeeting Remote Desktop Sharing icon on the taskbar, and choose Turn Off Remote Sharing from the shortcut menu. To permanently remove Remote Desktop Sharing, start NetMeeting, choose Remote Desktop Sharing from the Tools menu, and clear the Enable Remote Desktop Sharing On This Computer check box.

Controlling a Computer at Your Workplace ⊕ NEW FEATURE

Wouldn't it be great to sit at your home computer—wearing your pajamas and slippers if you want—and actually be able to use your computer at work? If your work computer is running Windows XP Professional or Windows XP Server, you can use the Remote Desktop Connection to take control of your work computer and get your work done just as if you were sitting in your office.

Connect to the Computer

① Use your usual method to connect to your office network.

② Choose Remote Desktop Connection from the Communications submenu of the Start menu to display the Remote Desktop Connection dialog box.

③ Type the name or IP address of your work computer.

> **!** **TIP:** The computer you're connecting to must be configured to allow the Remote Desktop Connection, and the user name with which you log on must be authorized to create the Remote Desktop Connection. If you're the authorized user, you can't connect with a blank password—you must have a valid password.

> **!** **TIP:** To make changes to the way you're connected, to optimize the connection for speed, and to make resources on your home computer available to the remote computer, click the Options button in the Connect dialog box. To learn about different settings and ways of using the Remote Desktop Connection, click the Help button in the Connect dialog box.

Remote Desktop Connection

Remote Desktop **Connection**

Computer: saturn

Connect | Cancel | Help | Options >>

④ Click Connect.

Log On to Windows

Windows XP
Professional
Copyright © 1985-2001
Microsoft Corporation
Microsoft

User name: Jerry Joyce
Password: ••••••••

OK | Cancel | Options >>

⑤ Type the user name and password that you use at the office and, if the computer is part of a domain, the domain name.

⑥ Click OK.

Control the Computer

1 Use the remote Desktop of your work computer just as if you were sitting at your desk in the office.

2 Click to resize the remote Desktop.

3 Switch between programs on your home computer and your work computer. You can copy and paste items, such as text or graphics, between programs, regardless of which computer each program is on.

Your Desktop

Remote Desktop

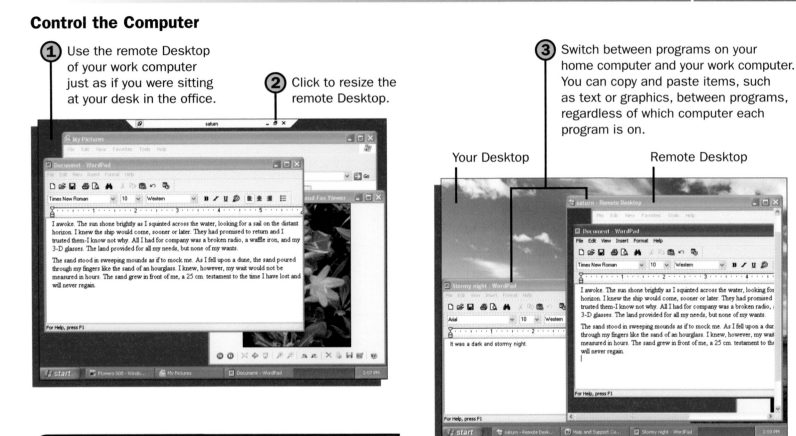

4 When you've finished, open the Start menu, and choose to log off or disconnect.

CAUTION: If someone else is logged on to the remote computer when you log on, the other person will be logged off, which could possibly cause some loss of data.

Connecting to a Network Using a Modem

If you want to connect to a business network over a phone line, you can use Dial-Up Networking to make the connection and to log on to the company's network. You'll be required to establish an account that lets you access resources on the network, and you'll need the proper permissions to connect. Be sure to get all the information you need from the company's network administrator before you connect. Every company has its own security settings and policies, so you'll need those details for the proper configuration.

> ✋ **CAUTION:** If you choose to save your user name and password so that anyone can use them, you're leaving the network vulnerable to unauthorized access and possible damage, all in your name. To protect access, save the name only for yourself, and use a password when you first log on to your computer. Also make sure that your computer is free of viruses. When you connect directly to a large network, your computer is probably the weakest link in the network's security.

Create the Dial-Up Connection

1 Choose New Connection Wizard from the Communications submenu of the Start menu, and click Next to start the wizard.

2 Click the Connect To The Network At My Workplace option, and click Next.

3 Click the Dial-Up Connection option, and click Next.

4 Type a name for the connection, and click Next.

5 Type the phone number for calling the network, and click Next. Click Finish to create the connection.

Connect

① Point to Connect To on the Start menu, and choose the connection to your work computer from the submenu to display the Connect dialog box.

② Enter your assigned user name and password to connect to the remote network.

④ Click Dial.

③ If you don't want to enter your user name and password each time you connect, select this check box, and then click the Me Only option. To save the information so that anyone who uses the computer can use your name and password, click the Anyone Who Uses This Computer option.

⑤ Wait to be connected, and then use the connection just as you use any network connection.

⑥ When you've finished, click the connection icon in the notification area of the task bar to display the Status dialog box. Click Disconnect.

! TIP: What you're able to do on the network depends on the design of the system you're connected to. If you run into any problems accessing the resources you need, contact the network administrator for advice.

! TIP: If you need to make the connection through an operator, click View Network Connections in the Network Tasks list in My Network Places, specify the connection, and choose Operator-Assisted Dialing from the Advanced menu.

Connecting to a Network over the Internet

To connect to your network over the Internet, you can use a VPN (Virtual Private Network), which provides a secure connection between your computer and the network. The computer you connect to must be configured as a VPN server and must be connected to the Internet. Before you connect, verify that you have the correct name of the host computer and the correct user name and password that have been assigned to you.

Create the VPN Connection

1 Choose New Connection Wizard from the Communications submenu of the Start menu, and click Next to start the wizard.

2 Click the Connect To The Network At My Workplace option, and click Next.

3 Click the Virtual Private Network Connection option, and click Next.

4 Type a name for the connection, and click Next.

5 Specify whether or not you want Windows XP to dial the Internet connection whenever you want to connect to the VPN. If you want Windows XP to do the dialing, click the connection to the Internet in the list, and click Next.

6 Type the host name or the IP address that you were provided with by the person who administers the host computer, and click Next. Click Finish to create the connection.

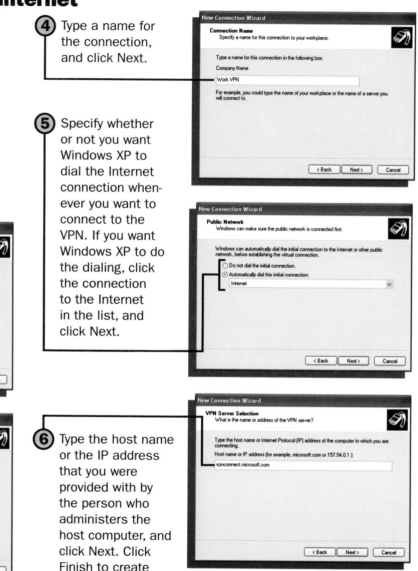

Connect

① If you chose not to have your Internet connection made automatically when the VPN connection is made, and if you're not currently connected, connect to the Internet. Point to Connect To on the Start menu, and choose the connection to your work computer from the submenu to display the Connect dialog box.

② Enter your assigned user name and password to connect to the remote network.

④ Click Connect.

③ If you don't want to enter your user name and password each time you connect, select this check box, and then click the Me Only option. To save the information so that anyone who uses the computer can use your name and password, click the Anyone Who Uses This Computer option.

> **! TIP:** Sometimes the configuration used by an ISP (Internet Service Provider) can interfere when you're creating a VPN connection. If you encounter any problems, check with your ISP to determine whether you need to change any of your settings.

⑤ Wait for the connection to be established, and then use it just as you use any other network connection.

⑥ When you've finished, click the connection icon for the VPN in the notification area of the taskbar to display the Status dialog box. Click Disconnect.

> **! TIP:** Although a VPN connection provides a direct and secure connection to the network, you're still subject to all the slowdowns that you might experience whenever you use the Internet, including a slow connection to your service provider, slow performance by your service provider, a general slowdown of the Internet, and poor performance from the VPN server. If you're planning to transfer large files, be prepared to wait!

Connecting to Your Computer from Another Location

If you want to connect to your own computer from another computer and establish a network connection so that you can transfer or use files, you can turn your computer into a small version of a dial-up network server. To do so, you create an incoming connection and allow only authorized users to connect to your computer.

Create an Incoming Connection

(1) Choose New Connection Wizard from the Communications submenu of the Start menu, and click Next to start the wizard.

(2) Click the Set Up An Advanced Connection option, and click Next.

(3) Click the Accept Incoming Connections option, and click Next.

(4) Specify the device (usually your modem) that you'll be using.

(5) Click the Do Not Allow Virtual Private Connections option.

(6) Select the check boxes for the users who are allowed access to your computer. (Only authorized users of the computer can connect.)

(7) Click Next, click Next again in the Network Software page of the wizard, and click Finish to create the incoming connection.

11 Setting Up

❋ NEW FEATURE

One of the things that usually takes all the fun out of buying a new computer is having to set up all over again the files and settings that took such a long time to get exactly right on your old computer. Well, we have good news for you! You can transfer your files and settings easily and quickly with the help of a wizard that walks you through the process. If you choose to transfer the information over your network, you provide a few pieces of information and type a password, and the transfer happens automatically. If you use disks to transfer the information, just follow the instructions on the screen until the transfer is complete.

True to this section's title, you'll also find information about setting up dial-up Internet access so that you can explore the far reaches of the Web's vastness; setting up Outlook Express for sending and receiving e-mail messages, as well as for subscribing to newsgroups; setting up Fax Service so that you can send and receive faxes directly through your computer; setting up a printer that's attached to your computer; and setting up a network.

In addition, in this section we'll talk about adding or removing Microsoft Windows XP components or parts thereof, installing software programs, and adding hardware devices to your computer.

If these all sound like daunting tasks, rest assured that they're not. With the instructions on the pages that follow, and with help from the wonderful wizards of Microsoft, you'll sail right through them.

Transferring Files and Settings ⊛ NEW FEATURE

If you said "bye-bye" to your old computer and went out and bought a new super-duper computer loaded with Windows XP, you'll be glad to know that you can transfer your files and all sorts of settings from the old computer to the new one. You don't have to set everything up again! You can transfer your settings, including those for Outlook Express, Internet Explorer, and your dial-up connections, by running the Files And Settings Transfer Wizard on both your old and new computers.

Set Up the Computers

1 On the new computer, choose the Files And Settings Transfer Wizard from the System Tools submenu of the Start menu.

2 On the new computer, step through the beginning part of the wizard, completing the information below, and then stopping when the wizard tells you to stop. Specify that

- This the new computer.
- You're going to use the Windows XP CD on the old computer. If you don't have the CD, use the option to create a copy of the wizard on a floppy disk.

3 On the old computer, insert the Windows XP CD, and, when it starts, choose Perform Additional Tasks from the menu that appears. On the next menu, choose Transfer Files And Settings to start the Files And Settings Transfer Wizard. Step through the wizard, specifying

- That this is the old computer.
- Whether you're going to transfer the file using a serial transfer cable, your network (which is the easiest way), a multitude of floppy disks, or a removable drive or network drive.

> ⓘ **TIP:** The network-connection option is available only when both computers are running the Files And Settings Transfer Wizard and when both computers are properly connected to your network.

Transfer the Information

① On the old computer, specify whether you want to copy files, settings, or both, and whether you want to select which files and settings are to be copied.

! TIP: Some files and settings can't be transferred. After you've completed the transfer procedure but before you click Finish, note any comments about files or settings that weren't transferred successfully.

③ If you're transferring the information over your network, write down the password that's displayed on the new computer, type it in the Password dialog box on the old computer, and click OK. The transfer will take place automatically.

④ If you're using disks, on the new computer, click Next. Click the Floppy Drive Or Other Removable Media option, and click Next. Follow the instructions on the screen to switch disks.

② Click Next. If you're using disks, follow the instructions on the screen, and switch disks when prompted to do so.

! TIP: If you're using a serial transfer cable, you'll need to establish the connection on both computers before you start gathering information from your old computer. Follow the directions in the wizard to establish the connection.

⑤ Click Finish when the transfer is complete.

Adding or Removing Windows Components

When Windows XP is installed on your computer, some—but not all—of its components are included in the installation. If any components you need haven't been installed, you can add them, and, by the same token, if there are components you never use, you can remove them from your system to save disk space.

> **! TIP:** A shaded check box indicates that only some of the items in the group will be installed. Use the Details button to modify which items are to be installed.

Add or Remove a Component Group

(1) Save any documents you're working on, and close all your running programs.

(2) Choose Control Panel from the Start menu, and click the Add Or Remove Programs category to display the Add Or Remove Programs dialog box.

(3) Click Add/Remove Windows Components to start the Windows Components Wizard.

(4) On the Windows Components page of the wizard, clear a check box to remove an entire component, or select a check box to add all the items in a component group.

> **SEE ALSO:** For information about updating existing Windows components or adding components that have recently been released, see "Updating Your System" on page 218.

> **! TIP:** You can install additional components and utilities from other sources. On the Windows XP CD, in the Valueadd folder, you'll find the Setup program for Windows Backup—a program for backing up and safeguarding your files. If you buy Microsoft Plus! For Windows XP, you'll find that it contains numerous additional components and utilities. And you can find many other items at the Windows Update Web site.

Add or Remove an Item in a Component Group

① Click the component group that contains the item you want to add or remove.

③ Clear a selected check box to remove that item, or select a cleared check box to add that item.

② Click Details. If the button is grayed (unavailable), there are no individual items to be managed, so you must either add or remove the entire component.

④ If the Details button is available when you select an item, click the button.

⑥ Click OK.

⑤ Select or clear the check boxes for the individual items you want to add or remove. Click OK when you've finished.

! TIP: To install new fonts on your system, open the Control Panel, click the Appearance And Themes category, and click Fonts in the See Also list in the Appearance And Themes window. In the Fonts window, choose Install New Font from the File menu.

⑦ Click Next. If prompted, insert the Windows XP CD into its drive, or specify the location of the installation folder. Click Finish to close the Windows Components Wizard, and click OK if prompted to restart the computer to complete the installation.

Installing a Software Program

Almost every software program contains its own installation program, which copies the required files to the computer's hard disk and tells Windows XP which files are installed, where they are, and what they do.

Install a Program

(1) Close all your running programs. If you're installing from a CD, insert the CD into its drive, follow the instructions that appear on the screen, and skip steps 2 through 5.

(2) If the CD didn't start, or if you're installing from a different drive or from a network location, choose Control Panel from the Start menu, and click the Add Or Remove Programs category to display the Add Or Remove Programs dialog box.

TIP: You can also install a program by double-clicking its *setup.exe* or *install.exe* program in a folder window.

TIP: Some programs are only partially installed until you use them for the first time. When you first choose one of these programs from the Start menu, you'll be asked whether you want to install it. You'll see this request if you chose Install On First Use when you installed the program.

(4) Click CD Or Floppy. Insert the CD or the installation disk into its drive, and click Next.

(5) If the Setup or installation program is found, click Finish. If not, click Browse, locate the Setup or installation program on a different drive or in a network folder, and click Finish.

(3) Click Add New Programs.

(6) Follow the Setup or installation program's instructions, and close the Add Or Remove dialog box when the installation is complete.

Setting Up Dial-Up Internet Access

Many ISPs (Internet Service Providers) supply installation CDs or other setup disks, and all you have to do is insert the CD or the disks into the appropriate drive and follow the instructions on the screen. However, if you don't have the installation materials, you can easily set up your connection manually.

Set Up a Connection

(1) Choose New Connection Wizard from the Communications submenu of the Start menu, and click Next to start the wizard.

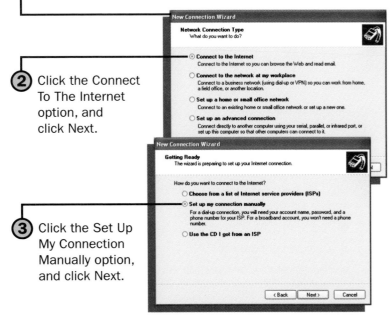

(2) Click the Connect To The Internet option, and click Next.

(3) Click the Set Up My Connection Manually option, and click Next.

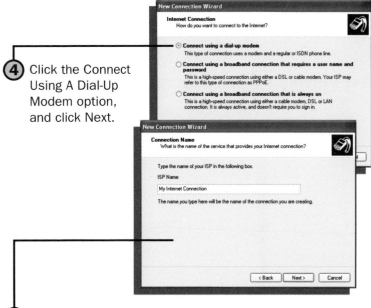

(4) Click the Connect Using A Dial-Up Modem option, and click Next.

(5) Continue through the wizard, specifying the following:

- A descriptive name for the connection
- The access phone number
- Your user name for connecting to the ISP
- Your password for connecting to the ISP
- Whether this account may be used by everyone who uses the computer
- Whether this is your default connection
- Whether you want the Internet firewall turned on for security.

TIP: To set up access through MSN (The Microsoft Network) or through another provider suggested by Microsoft, click the Choose From A List Of Internet Service Providers (ISPs) option instead of clicking the option to set up the connection manually.

SEE ALSO: For information about using a firewall to protect your Internet access, see "Configuring an Internet Firewall" on page 205.

Setting Up Outlook Express

When you first set up Windows XP, you probably set up your e-mail account at the same time. However, if you didn't set up the account, or if you want to add newsgroups or another e-mail account, you can easily make changes to the Outlook Express setup.

> **! TIP: In case you're wondering, POP3 is Post Office Protocol 3, IMAP is Internet Message Access Protocol, HTTP is Hypertext Transfer Protocol, and NNTP is Network News Transfer Protocol.**

Set Up Your E-Mail Account

① Choose Outlook Express from the Start menu.

Internet Connection Wizard

Your Name

When you send e-mail, your name will appear in the From field of the outgoing message. Type your name as you would like it to appear.

Display name: Marianne Moon

For example: John Smith

[< Back] [Next >] [Cancel]

Internet Connection Wizard

Internet E-mail Address

Your e-mail address is the address other people use to send e-mail messages to you.

E-mail address: moonjoyceresourc@hotmail.com

For example: someone@microsoft.com

[< Back] [Next >] [Cancel]

② Step through the Internet Connection Wizard that appears, specifying the following:

- Your name as you want it displayed in your e-mail
- Your e-mail address
- The type of incoming mail server (HTTP, POP3, or IMAP)
- The addresses of the incoming and outgoing e-mail servers, if they haven't already been supplied
- Your e-mail account name (usually the same as your e-mail address) and your password

> **SEE ALSO: For information about transferring your Outlook Express settings and messages from another computer, see "Transferring Files and Settings" on page 164.**
>
> **For information about creating an Internet connection to your ISP (Internet Service Provider), see "Setting Up Dial-Up Internet Access" on page 169.**

Add an Account

1 In Outlook Express, choose Accounts from the Tools menu to display the Internet Accounts dialog box.

2 Click Add, and choose Mail from the submenu that appears. Step through the Internet Connection Wizard to add the e-mail account.

3 Click Add again, and choose News from the submenu to start the Internet Connection Wizard. Step through the wizard, specifying the following:

- Your name as you want it to appear in the newsgroups
- Your e-mail address
- The address of the news server
- Whether you need to log on to use the server, and, if so, your logon name and password

SEE ALSO: For information about using Outlook Express, see "Sending E-Mail" on page 54 and "Subscribing to Newsgroups" on page 61.

TIP: Gather up all your account information from your ISP before you set up the e-mail account. Mail protocols and server names can be complex and confusing.

Setting Up for Faxing

If your computer has a fax modem, you can use Fax Service, which allows you to send and receive faxes through your computer. Before you can use Fax Service, you'll need to provide some personal information that can be used on the fax cover page. You'll also need to enter your identification number for Fax Service and set options for the way you want your faxes to be sent and received.

Set the Options

1 Choose Fax Console from the Fax submenu of the Start menu, and choose Configure Fax from the Tools menu to start the Fax Configuration Wizard. Click Next to start the wizard.

2 Enter your personal information, and click Next.

TIP: The TSID is the Transmitting Station Identifier and is usually sent along with the fax so that the recipient can identify the source of the fax. In many locations, a TSID is required by law. The CSID is the Called Subscriber Identifier. This identification is sent back to the sending fax device to confirm your identity, and it's also used in a log that records received faxes.

TIP: The Fax printer is used exclusively to send faxes, and it can't be shared, so you can't share your fax modem with other computers on your network. A fax modem can, however, be shared through a Windows XP Professional computer.

3 Make sure the correct fax device is specified.

4 Select this check box if you want to send faxes from your computer.

5 Select this check box if you want to receive faxes on your computer.

6 If you want to receive faxes, click an option to specify whether the faxes are to be received manually or automatically. If you specify automatic receiving, designate the number of rings before the modem answers the call.

7 Complete the wizard, specifying the following:
- The TSID
- The CSID
- Whether every received fax should be printed by a specific printer
- Whether a copy of the fax is to be stored in a specific folder

SEE ALSO: For information about installing Fax Service if it isn't already installed, see "Adding or Removing Windows Components" on page 166.

Setting Up a Printer

Windows XP might or might not detect your printer, depending on how and to what the printer is attached. Windows should detect and install any printer that's attached to your computer's USB (Universal Serial Bus) or infrared port. If the printer is attached to a parallel or serial port, however, Windows might not have detected the printer when it was installed, so you'll need tell Windows about it yourself.

SEE ALSO: For information about sharing your printer over a network, see "Share a Printer" on page 149.

Set Up a Printer

(1) If the printer came with an installation disk that's designed to work with Windows XP, follow the directions that came with the printer to run the installation program. The printer should then be installed correctly.

(2) If you don't have an installation disk, with the printer connected and turned on, choose Control Panel from the Start menu, click the Printers And Other Hardware category, and click the Add A Printer task. Click Next to start the Add Printer Wizard.

(3) Click the Local Printer Attached To This Computer option.

(4) Select this check box to have Windows XP look for the printer, and then click Next. If Windows doesn't detect the printer, click Next.

(6) Do either of the following:

- Select the manufacturer and model of the printer.

- Click Have Disk if you have a disk or a download of the required files. Use the Browse button to locate the files, and click OK.

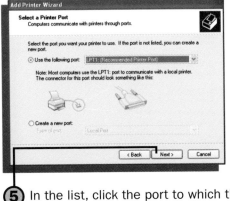

(7) Click Next, and complete the wizard, specifying the following:

- A name for the printer

- Whether this is your default printer

- Whether the printer is to be shared on your network, and, if so, the name it will display to the other computers

- Whether you want to print a test page to verify the setup

(5) In the list, click the port to which the printer is connected, and click Next.

Setting Up a Network

If your network hasn't already been set up, you can configure it easily. To do so, you first have to set up one of the computers as the network *host*. Then you configure the other computers on your network to be *clients* of the host.

Set Up the Host Computer

① With all your network connections in place and all the computers turned on, on the computer that will host your network, choose Network Setup Wizard from the Communications submenu of the Start menu, and click Next to start the wizard.

② Step through the wizard, specifying the following:

- That this computer connects directly to the Internet
- The connection you'll use to connect to the Internet
- A friendly description of the computer and a name for the computer
- A name for your workgroup

③ After confirming the configuration and clicking Next, wait for the computer to do a preliminary search of the network to identify the computers and shared items that are available.

⑤ Click Next, and follow the instructions to complete the wizard.

> **! TIP:** Be sure to set up your Internet connection on the host computer before you set up the network. Verify that all the computers that will be on the network have the proper network cards and cables and are turned on and operating correctly.

> **✋ CAUTION:** A network can have only one host. If you're adding a computer that's running Windows XP, and you want that computer to host an existing network that uses ICS (Internet Connection Sharing), you must disable ICS before you can set up your Windows XP computer as the host.

④ If a computer that will be part of the network isn't running Windows XP, do either of the following:

- Click the Create A Network Setup Disk option if you don't have a Windows XP CD.
- Click the Use My Windows XP CD option.

Set Up a Network Client

(1) Choose Network Setup Wizard from the Communications submenu of the Start menu, and click Next to start the wizard.

(2) If the computer isn't running Windows XP, insert the Windows XP CD and, when the CD starts, choose Perform Additional Tasks from the menu that appears. From the next menu, choose Set Up A Home Or Small Office Network.

(3) Step through the wizard, specifying the following:

- That this computer connects to the Internet through another computer or through a residential gateway

- A friendly description of the computer and a name for the computer

- A name for your workgroup

(4) After confirming the configuration and clicking Next, wait for the computer to search your network, and then complete the wizard.

! TIP: If you aren't using the Windows XP CD, and if you created a setup disk, place the disk in the client computer's disk drive, choose Run from the Start menu, type a:netsetup and press Enter.

✋ CAUTION: Choose your host computer carefully. If you're sharing an Internet connection with other computers on the network, the host computer must be turned on whenever any of the other computers need to access the Internet.

Adding Hardware

In most cases, when you install a piece of hardware, Windows XP detects it, configures it, and installs the necessary software drivers. Sometimes, however, Windows doesn't detect the hardware device, which means that you'll have to install it manually. When a device isn't detected, it's usually because Windows doesn't have the necessary software drivers, so you'll need to obtain that software from the manufacturer before you can install the device.

Set Up the Hardware

(1) If the hardware has been properly installed on the computer but Windows XP doesn't recognize it, shut down Windows and then restart it to see whether Windows has detected the hardware now.

(2) If Windows still hasn't detected the hardware, open the Control Panel, and click Printers And Other Hardware. Click Add Hardware in the See Also list to start the Add Hardware Wizard. Click Next to start the wizard.

(3) Click the Yes, I Have Already Connected The Hardware option, and click Next.

(4) Review the list of installed items. If your hardware is listed, it has already been installed, but there might be a problem. Double-click the item to see whether there's any trouble-shooting information about it and to complete the wizard.

(5) If your hardware isn't listed, double-click Add A New Hardware Device. Click the Search For And Install The Hardware Automatically option, and click Next. If the hardware is detected, Windows should install it for you.

(6) If Windows doesn't detect the hardware, click Next, and double-click the type of device.

(7) Do either of the following:

- Click the manufacturer and model.

- Click Have Disk if you have a disk or a download of the required files. Use the Browse button to locate the files, and click OK.

(8) Click Next, and complete the wizard.

12 Customizing

✱ NEW FEATURE
✱ NEW FEATURE

✱ NEW FEATURE

With Microsoft Windows XP installed, you can customize just about everything on your computer to make it look and work exactly the way you want it to. If the new look of Windows XP doesn't appeal to you, you can revert to the classic Windows interface, you can design your own look with elements from both styles, or you can change the look to that of a Web page. You can customize your Desktop with a color, a picture, or Web content that can be updated on a specific schedule. You can change the size and color of almost everything; set items to open with one click instead of two; rearrange or hide the taskbar, toolbars, Start menu, and Desktop items; and create your own toolbars.

You can use a single window in which to open all your folders, or use a separate window for each folder if you prefer; you can choose the details—date, author, and so on—that you want to be shown in your folder windows; and you can customize your folder windows with colors and pictures. You can change the way you log on for increased security, change the picture that Windows assigns to your user account, and even change the way a CD starts depending on its content.

If you have any problems with your vision, hearing, or manual dexterity—or if you simply want to try a different way of working— you can use some innovative tools: press key combinations one key at a time instead of simultaneously, use high-contrast color schemes or the Magnifier tool for better visibility, control mouse movements with the numeric keypad on your keyboard, specify visual cues to replace the computer's beeps, or type your text on the On-Screen Keyboard.

Changing the Overall Look

Windows XP has its own very new look, but if it doesn't appeal to you, you can change whatever you don't like about it—the colors, the fonts, and so on. If you yearn for the familiarity of the old classic Windows look, a few mouse-clicks do away with the new and bring back the old. Can't decide? How about a combination of the old and the new, or a design of your own?

> **TIP:** Your Theme list might contain a variety of different themes, depending on whether you installed Windows XP as an upgrade, whether you installed the Microsoft Plus! For Windows XP package, or whether you downloaded themes. To download themes, choose More Themes Online from the Theme list.

Switch to the Classic Windows Look

(1) Right-click a blank spot on the Desktop, and choose Properties from the shortcut menu to display the Display Properties dialog box.

(2) Click the Themes tab.

(3) Click the down arrow in the Theme box, and click Windows Classic in the list.

(4) Click Apply, and wait for the theme to be applied.

> **SEE ALSO:** For information about switching the Start menu to the classic Windows layout, see "Customizing the Start Menu" on page 184.

> **TIP:** To return to the original Windows XP look after you've made changes, click Windows XP in the Theme list.

Customize the Look ⊕ NEW FEATURE

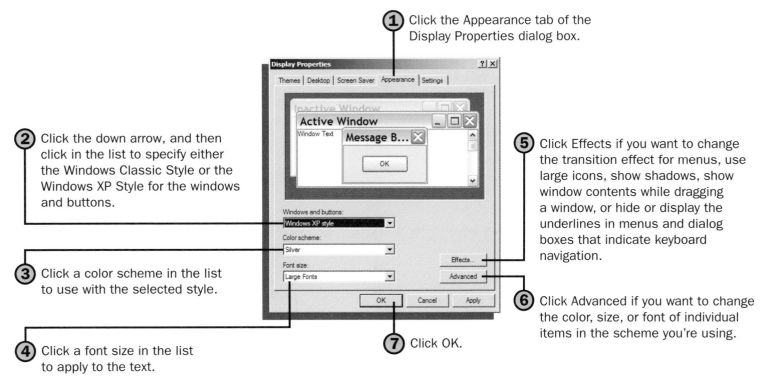

(1) Click the Appearance tab of the Display Properties dialog box.

(2) Click the down arrow, and then click in the list to specify either the Windows Classic Style or the Windows XP Style for the windows and buttons.

(3) Click a color scheme in the list to use with the selected style.

(4) Click a font size in the list to apply to the text.

(5) Click Effects if you want to change the transition effect for menus, use large icons, show shadows, show window contents while dragging a window, or hide or display the underlines in menus and dialog boxes that indicate keyboard navigation.

(6) Click Advanced if you want to change the color, size, or font of individual items in the scheme you're using.

(7) Click OK.

(!) TIP: The ClearType option in the Effects dialog box smoothes the edges of screen fonts and can dramatically improve the readability of text on a flat screen, such as that of a portable computer. The ClearType option might not work quite as well on a standard CRT monitor.

(✋) CAUTION: If you modify a theme and then choose another theme, you'll lose all your changes. To preserve your changes, click the Save As button on the Themes tab, type a name for your theme, and click Save.

Customizing the Desktop

Your physical desktop—whether it's oak, glass, or some sort of composite—always looks the same (assuming it's visible under that pile of paper in your "paperless office"). Your Windows XP Desktop, on the other hand, can change dramatically. You can paint it any color you want, and it can display a picture. You can hide all the standard Desktop icons or display the ones you need. Keep experimenting until you find the look you like.

Use a Background Color

① Right-click a blank spot on the Desktop, choose Properties from the shortcut menu, and click the Desktop tab of the Display Properties dialog box.

③ Specify the color you want for your Desktop.

④ Click Apply.

② Click None in the Background list.

> **SEE ALSO:** For information about adding Web content to your Desktop, see "Creating a Custom Desktop Background" on page 182.

> **TIP:** If you add Web content to your Desktop, your Desktop icons will use the background color as the background for their text. If no Web content is displayed, the background for the text is transparent.

Use a Picture

① In the Background list, click the name of the picture you want.

② If the picture you want isn't listed, click Browse, locate and select a picture, and click Open.

④ Click Apply.

③ In the Position list, click

- Center to place a single copy of the picture in the center of the Desktop.
- Tile to repeat the image to fill the Desktop.
- Stretch to scale the image to fit the Desktop. (Note that a scaled image might be distorted or its quality deteriorated.)

Display and Customize the Desktop Icons

1 In the Display Properties dialog box, click Customize Desktop.

2 On the General tab of the Desktop Items dialog box, select the check boxes for the icons you want on your Desktop and clear the check boxes for the ones you don't want.

3 To change the appearance of an icon, select the icon.

4 Click Change Icon.

8 Click OK.

7 Click OK.

5 In the Change Icon dialog box, click the icon you want.

6 Click OK.

TRY THIS: In the Change Icon dialog box, click the Browse button and open the *moricon.dll* file in the System32 subfolder of the Windows folder. If you don't like any of those icons, click the Browse button again and open the *shell32.dll* file in the same folder.

Creating a Custom Desktop Background

You can place photographs, Web content, and various other items on your Desktop. Although any windows you use will always be on top of this content, they're still active, so you can move and resize the items, or have Web pages update on a preset schedule.

Add Web Content

1 Right-click a blank spot on the Desktop, choose Properties from the shortcut menu, and, on the Desktop tab of the Display Properties dialog box, click the Customize Desktop button.

2 On the Web tab of the Desktop Items dialog box, click New.

3 In the list, click the item you want to add, or specify its source:

- Click Visit Gallery to download free Web components.

- Type or paste the address of a Web site in the Location box.

- Click Browse, and locate pictures, HTML documents, or offline Web pages that you've saved on your computer.

4 Click OK, and then click OK again to close the Display Properties dialog box.

5 Move the mouse pointer over an item until the title bar appears. Drag the title bar to move the item, or drag an edge to resize it.

Displaying and Arranging the Toolbars

The taskbar and the toolbars are indispensable tools for working efficiently in Windows XP. If you want, you can rearrange them so that they're tailored even more closely to your working style. For example, you can change the size of a toolbar or the taskbar, and you can "dock" either at any of the four sides of your screen. You can also "float" the toolbars—but not the taskbar—anywhere on your Desktop.

> **TIP:** The New Toolbar command creates a toolbar that displays the contents of the folder you specify.

Display a Toolbar

1 Right-click a blank spot on the taskbar, and, if there's a check mark next to the Lock The Taskbar command on the shortcut menu, click the command to unlock the taskbar.

2 Right-click a blank spot on the taskbar, point to Toolbars on the shortcut menu, and choose the toolbar you want to display.

Move It

1 Drag a toolbar onto the Desktop and then to any of the four sides of the screen to dock it there. Drag the inside border of the toolbar to resize it.

2 Point to the name of the toolbar, and drag it onto the Desktop to create a floating toolbar. Drag a border of the toolbar to resize the toolbar.

Customizing the Start Menu

The Start menu is your main resource for organizing your programs, files, and so on, and getting your work done in Windows XP. You can customize the Start menu in several ways: you can change its new Windows XP look so that it looks like the Start menu in previous versions of Windows; you can modify the way items are displayed on the Start menu and its various submenus; and you can add items to or delete items from the main part of the Start menu and from the All Programs submenus.

Choose and Customize the Style ⊙ NEW FEATURE

(1) Right-click the Start button, and choose Properties from the shortcut menu to display the Taskbar And Start Menu Properties dialog box.

(7) On the Advanced tab, select this check box if you want submenus to open when you point to them (rather than when you click them).

(8) Select this check box if you want newly installed programs to be highlighted on the Start menu.

(9) Select check boxes and click options to specify whether and how various items are to be included on the Start menu.

(2) Click an option to specify the style you want for the Start menu.

(3) Click Customize.

(4) Specify whether you want to see large or small icons on the Start menu.

(5) Specify how many recently used programs you want listed.

(6) Select the check boxes if you want your Internet browser and e-mail program listed, and, if so, specify the programs.

(10) Select this check box if you want an item with a submenu that lists your most recently used documents to be displayed.

(11) Click OK, and then click OK again to close the Taskbar And Start Menu Properties dialog box.

Add or Remove a Start Menu Program ⊕ NEW FEATURE

(1) Open the Start menu, locate the program you want to add (from one of the All Programs submenus or from a folder), and right-click it.

Add a Shortcut to an Item to the Start Menu

(1) Locate the item, right-click it, point to Send To on the shortcut menu, and choose Desktop to create a shortcut on the Desktop to the item.

(2) Choose Pin To Start Menu from the shortcut menu.

(3) Right-click a program that has been "pinned" to the Start menu, and choose Unpin From Start Menu from the shortcut menu to remove the program.

TRY THIS: Drag a shortcut onto a submenu of the All Programs menu. Right-click the shortcut, and rename it. Drag any other items you want onto the submenu. Right-click anywhere in a submenu, and choose Sort By Name to organize that submenu.

(2) Drag the shortcut from the Desktop onto the Start button, and, when the Start menu opens, drag the shortcut to the location you want.

Customizing the Taskbar ❀ NEW FEATURE

The taskbar is a really handy navigation device, and you can make it even more efficient by customizing it to your work habits. You can specify which items are displayed on it and how they're displayed, and you can even hide the taskbar when you aren't using it and have it reappear when you need it.

> ❋ **NEW FEATURE: As more and more programs place icons in the notification area of the taskbar, it's often difficult to find the ones you need and use. Hiding the inactive icons makes the ones you use easy to find. Anytime you need to access one of the hidden icons, just click the Show Hidden Icons button at the left of the notification area.**

Customize the Taskbar

① Right-click a blank spot on the taskbar, and choose Properties from the shortcut menu to display the Taskbar And Start Menu Properties dialog box.

② Select this check box to prevent the taskbar from being moved to a new location or to prevent toolbars from being resized.

③ Select this check box to hide the taskbar when you're not using it. The taskbar will reappear when you move the mouse to whichever side of the screen contains the taskbar.

④ Select this check box to prevent other windows from obscuring the taskbar.

⑤ Select this check box to have similar items grouped in one button when the taskbar is crowded.

⑥ Select this check box to display the Quick Launch toolbar.

⑦ Select this check box to have the clock appear in the notification area of the taskbar.

⑧ Select this check box to hide seldom-used icons in the notification area of the taskbar.

⑨ Click Customize to specify which icons are always displayed, which are never displayed, and which are hidden when inactive.

⑩ Click OK.

Changing the Logon ● NEW FEATURE

The standard—and the simplest—way to log on to Windows XP is to click your name on the Welcome screen, and, if you've set up a password, to type your password. If you're a traditionalist and/or if you want to boost the security of your system, you can switch to the traditional logon—that is, you type both your user name and your password. When you choose to use the traditional logon, though, you disable Fast User Switching (the ability to allow someone else to log on to your computer without your having to log off).

Change to the Traditional Logon

(1) Choose Control Panel from the Start menu, click the User Accounts category, and then click the Change The Way Users Log On Or Off task to display the User Accounts window.

(2) Clear this check box.

(3) Click Apply Options, and then close the User Accounts window and the Control Panel window.

Log On

(1) Choose Log Off from the Start menu, and confirm that you do want to log off.

(2) In the Log On To Windows dialog box that appears, type your user name if it isn't already displayed.

(4) Click OK.

(3) Type your password. If you haven't created a password, leave the box blank.

> **CAUTION:** As you should always do whenever you're making systemwide changes, verify that you're the only person who's currently logged on to the computer.

Customizing Your Folders

Working in Windows XP means that you work with folders. To adapt the folders to your working style, you can customize them so that they look and work in exactly the way you like. Some of the changes you make apply to all your folders and other changes apply to the single folder that's open. In some cases, you can first apply the changes to a single folder and then, if you want, apply them to all your folders.

Change the Way All the Folders Work

1 Choose My Computer from the Start menu, and choose Folder Options from the Tools menu to display the Folder Options dialog box.

2 Click the first option to have frequently used tasks displayed on the left side of the folder. Click the second option to have only the contents of the folder displayed.

3 Click the first option if you want all your folders to open in the same window—that is, when you open one folder from another folder, the second folder's content replaces that of the first folder in the window. Click the second option if you want to use a separate window for each folder that you open.

4 Click the first option if you want to click only once to open an item in a folder. Click the second option if you want to double-click to open an item. If you chose the first option, specify how you want the icon text to be underlined.

TIP: To learn more about the function of each option on the View tab, click the Help button at the top right of the dialog box, and then click the option.

TRY THIS: To apply the same view to all your folders, select a view from the Views button, choose Folder Options from the Tools menu, and, on the View tab, click the Apply To All Folders button. Click OK.

5 Click the View tab.

7 Click OK.

6 Select check boxes for the options you want and clear check boxes for the options you don't want.

Change the Look of a Folder

1 Open the folder you want to customize, and choose Customize This Folder from the View menu to display the folder's Properties dialog box.

2 On the Customize tab, specify the predominant type of file this folder contains.

3 Select this check box if you want any subfolders in this folder to use the same layout.

4 Click Choose Picture, and select a picture to be displayed on the folder when you're viewing the folder in Thumbnails view.

5 Click Change Icon to specify a different icon for the folder.

6 Click OK

Books Properties

General | Sharing | Customize

What kind of folder do you want?
Use this folder type as a template:
Documents (for any file type)

☐ Also apply this template to all subfolders

Folder pictures
For Thumbnails view, you can put a picture on this folder to remind you of the contents.

Preview:

Choose Picture...
Restore Default

Folder icons
For all views except Thumbnails, you can change the standard "folder" icon to another icon.

Change Icon...

OK | Cancel | Apply

Change the Content that's Shown

1 Choose Choose Details from the View menu to display the Choose Details dialog box.

2 Select check boxes for the details you want to be shown in the folder window and clear check boxes for the details that don't need to be shown.

3 Use the appropriate button to change the order of the items or to show or hide them.

4 Specify the width in pixels of the column for the selected item.

5 Click OK when you've finished.

Choose Details

Select the details you want to display for the files in this folder.

Details:
☑ Name
☑ Size
☑ Type
☑ Date Modified
☑ Date Created
☐ Date Accessed
☐ Attributes
☐ Status
☐ Owner
☐ Author
☐ Title
☐ Subject
☐ Category
☐ Pages
☐ Comments

Move Up
Move Down
Show
Hide

Width of selected column (in pixels): 120

OK | Cancel

Changing the Way a CD Starts

When you insert a CD into your computer's CD drive, Windows detects the type of content on the CD—music or pictures, for example. Then Windows either asks you what you want to do with the CD or starts doing something without asking you, such as playing the music. If you want to make the decisions, you can let Windows know just how you want it to handle the various types of content on your CDs.

Set the AutoPlay

1 Choose My Computer from the Start menu, right-click the CD drive, and choose Properties from the shortcut menu to display the CD Properties dialog box.

2 Click the AutoPlay tab.

3 Specify the type of content.

4 Click one of the following options:

- Select An Action To Perform to specify an action that Windows will perform automatically

- Prompt Me Each Time To Choose An Action to see a dialog box listing the possible actions you can choose

5 If you selected the option to perform a specific action, select the action you want for the type of content you specified.

6 Select a different type of content, and repeat steps 4 and 5.

7 After you've specified all the actions, click OK.

Changing Your Account Picture ⊕ NEW FEATURE

Windows XP arbitrarily assigns your user account a picture, which seems to show up all the time. You see it when you log on or switch users, and there it is again every time you open the Start menu. If you don't like the picture or if you feel that it has no relevance to you, and if you have a picture that's just right, you can change the picture.

> **TIP:** The space where the user account picture goes is designed for a square picture, so, if your picture isn't square, you might want to crop it in Paint or in another photo-editing program to eliminate any blank space.

Change Your Picture

(1) Click the Start button to open the Start menu, and click your account picture.

(2) In the User Accounts window that appears, click the picture you want to use.

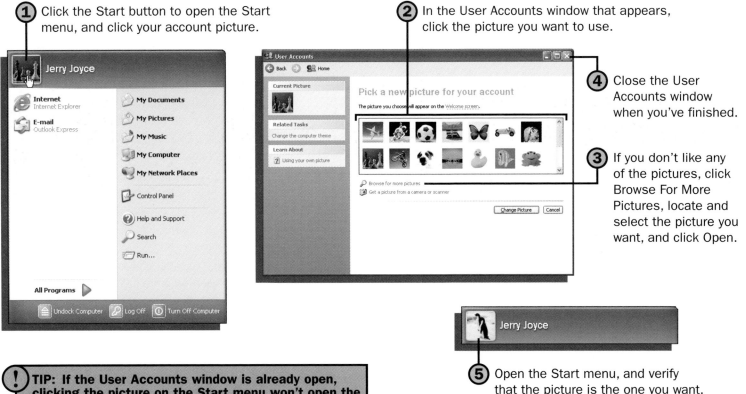

(4) Close the User Accounts window when you've finished.

(3) If you don't like any of the pictures, click Browse For More Pictures, locate and select the picture you want, and click Open.

(5) Open the Start menu, and verify that the picture is the one you want.

> **TIP:** If the User Accounts window is already open, clicking the picture on the Start menu won't open the window where you can change the picture. You'll need to click your account in the User Accounts window, and then click the Change My Picture task.

Using Alternative Ways of Working

Windows XP provides several tools that let you change the way you enter information into, or receive information from, the computer. These tools—although designed primarily for people who experience difficulty when typing, using the mouse, seeing details on the screen, or hearing sounds—can be used by anyone who'd like to try some different ways of working on the computer. For example, you can use the keyboard to execute mouse actions, or use the mouse or another pointing device for keyboard input. Some other tools that can help you customize keyboard input are described in the table below.

Set the Options

(1) Choose Control Panel from the Start menu, click the Accessibility Options category, and click Accessibility Options to display the Accessibility Properties dialog box.

(2) On the various tabs of the dialog box, select the check boxes for the options you want to use, as described in the table. Click the Settings button for each option you selected, and specify how you want the option to function. Click OK.

(3) On the General tab, specify whether you want the features you selected to be turned off after the computer has been idle for a set period of time, whether you want a warning message or a sound to be used when a feature is turned on or off, and whether you want the settings to be available when you log on and whenever any new users of the computer log on.

(4) Click OK to close the dialog box.

> **! TIP: You can use the Accessibility Wizard on the Accessibility submenu of the Start menu to provide a quick way to set up several tools at one time and to help you identify which tools you might want to use.**

Alternative Input Options

Feature	What it does
StickyKeys	Sets key combinations with the Alt, Ctrl, and Shift keys to be pressable one key at a time.
FilterKeys	Ignores repeated characters or too-rapid key presses.
ToggleKeys	Makes different sounds when you turn the Caps Lock, Num Lock, or Scroll Lock key on or off.
SoundSentry	Flashes a specified screen component when the system beeps.
ShowSounds	Displays text instead of sounds for programs that support this feature.
High Contrast	Sets the color scheme for Windows XP to High Contrast to improve the visibility of components.
Cursor Blink Rate	Sets the speed at which the cursor (the insertion point in WordPad, for example) blinks.
Cursor Width	Sets the width of the cursor in programs.
MouseKeys	Sets the numeric keypad to control mouse movements.
SerialKey devices	Provides support for alternative input devices.

Use More Tools

(1) On your keyboard, press the Windows key + U to display the Utility Manager and to start Narrator.

(2) Click the program you want to run.

(3) Click Start to start the program.

(4) Select or clear the check boxes to specify how you want the program to start.

(5) Click another program and start it and/or set its options.

(6) Click OK.

Use the On-Screen Keyboard to use the mouse or another pointing device to type your text.

Magnifier shows an enlarged view of the area in which you're working.

We received many new ideas in the competition. Initially we determining the winners, but once we re-examined our prio

The dream - WordPad
File Edit View Insert Format Help

We received many new ideas in the competition. Initially we had a very difficult time determining the winners, but once we re-examined our priorities, we came to unanimous conclusions. Our criteria were quite simple:

TIP: Use the Magnifier Settings dialog box to set both the magnification level and the way Magnifier tracks activities on the screen.

SEE ALSO: For information about using Narrator, see "Letting Your Computer Do the Talking" on page 106.

Using a Screen Saver

When you work at a computer, it's good for your eyes—and for your mental health—to take a break and look at something different once in a while. If you work with other people, you might not want them to be able to read your screen—albeit unintentionally—any time your computer is unattended. A screen saver can provide a nice little respite from your work as well as some privacy. To prevent anyone from using your computer—but still allow network access to it—when you're away from your desk, you can use the password option. You'll need to enter the password to end the screen saver when you're ready to get back to work.

Choose a Screen Saver

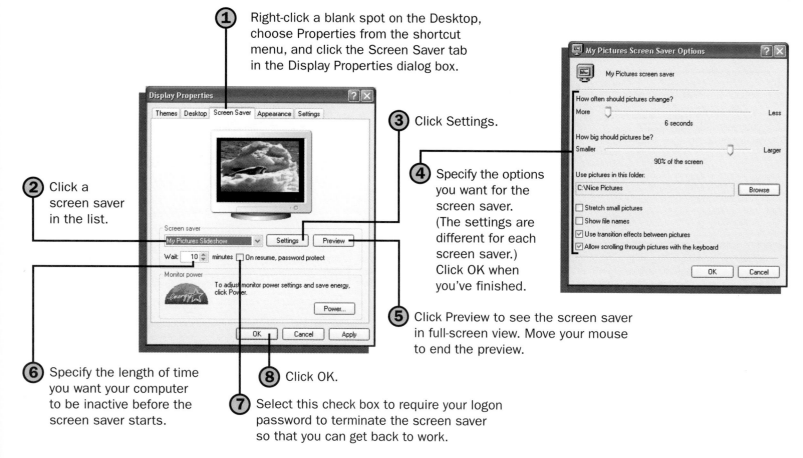

① Right-click a blank spot on the Desktop, choose Properties from the shortcut menu, and click the Screen Saver tab in the Display Properties dialog box.

③ Click Settings.

② Click a screen saver in the list.

④ Specify the options you want for the screen saver. (The settings are different for each screen saver.) Click OK when you've finished.

⑤ Click Preview to see the screen saver in full-screen view. Move your mouse to end the preview.

⑥ Specify the length of time you want your computer to be inactive before the screen saver starts.

⑧ Click OK.

⑦ Select this check box to require your logon password to terminate the screen saver so that you can get back to work.

13 Maintaining Security

✳ NEW FEATURE

✳ NEW FEATURE

✳ NEW FEATURE

In days of old, only the administrators of large corporate networks had to worry about computer security. These days, with the proliferation of computer viruses, constant connections to the Internet, home networks, and sophisticated hacking techniques used by an ever-growing cadre of snoops and pranksters, everyone should be vigilant. In this section you'll find valuable information about the various ways you can protect your files, your privacy on the Internet, and so on. If other people use your computer, you can protect your sensitive files from prying eyes by restricting *user rights,* by creating a password that protects the computer from unauthorized access, or by placing sensitive material in a compressed and *encrypted* folder. You can even lock your computer.

When you visit an Internet site that requests personal information, you can restrict the amount of information you provide by creating a special profile for that purpose. You can also control "cookies," those little files that Web sites use to keep track of your visits and preferences and that can compile a lot of personal information about you. We'll also show you how to configure an Internet *firewall* to create a high level of security. If several people use your computer (especially if any are children), you can use Content Advisor—a feature in Microsoft Internet Explorer—to restrict access to Internet sites that contain material you consider inappropriate. You can specify the acceptable level of material that may be accessed, or you can set up a password to allow access to restricted sites. To maintain your overall security, you need an effective password, and you should make a point of changing it occasionally.

Keeping Your Files Private

If other people use your computer, they can normally gain access to any of your files, including those in your My Documents folder. If your computer uses NTFS (the NT file system), however, you can keep your files private so that only you can access them when you log on to the computer.

Keep the My Documents Folder Private

1 Choose My Computer from the Start menu to open the My Computer window.

SEE ALSO: For information about NTFS, see "Know Your Rights, Know Your Format" on the facing page.

For information about creating a password, see "Setting Your Password" on page 198.

CAUTION: When you keep your My Documents folder private, you're also keeping all its subfolders private, including the My Music, My Pictures, Desktop, and Favorites subfolders. If you want to share any files from these folders, move them into the Shared Documents folder.

2 Right-click your Documents folder (it shows your logon name), and choose Sharing And Security from the shortcut menu.

3 On the Sharing tab, select this check box to keep the folder private.

5 If you're notified that you don't have a password, click Yes, and create a password.

4 Click OK.

Know Your Rights, Know Your Format

Microsoft Windows XP provides several tools to help you effectively maintain security on your computer system. One of the principal ways to maintain security is to assign specific rights to each user of the computer. These rights can range from simply being allowed to use the computer all the way up to having permission to make changes to the entire system. You assign user rights by assigning individual users to the appropriate group. Another way to maintain security is to use the built-in security of the NTFS file system, which provides extra security in Windows NT–based operating systems but isn't available in the Windows 95, Windows 98, or Windows Me (Millennium Edition) operating system. Your computer might or might not be using the NTFS system.

User Groups

What you're allowed to do on your computer depends on the user group of which you're a member—the Administrators group, the Limited group, or the Guest group. You can tell which group you've been assigned to by choosing Control Panel from the Start menu and clicking the User Accounts category.

Administrators have full control of the computer and can make any changes to the system, including adding or removing software, changing user accounts, and even modifying the Windows XP configuration. Members of the Administrators group are trusted to be able to use and modify the computer and its programs without causing problems.

Limited users can do most things that don't affect the overall setup of the computer, such as run programs, use and create files, and install some programs. Members of the Limited group can't install any program that accesses the Windows Registry, and can't add or remove users or make

substantial changes to Windows. Members of the Limited group might find that some older programs that weren't designed for use with Windows XP might not work correctly.

Guest users are people who don't have a user account on the computer. By logging on as a member of the Guest group, a user can work on the computer without being able to modify another user's settings. Guest users are quite limited in what they can do—they can run existing programs but can't install new programs or make any changes to Windows. By default, the Guest account is inactive and must be activated before it can be used. There is only one Guest account on the computer.

File Systems

The NTFS system provides extra security for your files. Some of this security is hidden, so you can't see it, but you can use it to keep your files private. Unless you're using NTFS, anyone who works on the computer can open the Documents And Settings folder and can access each user's My Documents folder, which is stored in the user's profile. Using NTFS, and with security settings in place, a user's My Documents folder can be accessed only when that user is logged on. NTFS isn't compatible with most other operating systems, however, so if your computer is running more than one operating system, you'll probably want to use the FAT or FAT32 file system instead of NTFS.

To see whether your computer uses NTFS, open My Computer, and click the hard disk. In the Details section of the window, you'll see the file system that's being used. If the computer has more than one hard disk, click each one and note the file system. For information about converting the hard disk to NTFS, see "Changing the Disk Format" on page 214.

Setting Your Password

Unless you create a password that allows you to gain entry to your user account, anyone can log on to your computer and access your files. If you want to protect the computer from unauthorized access, create a password that's easy for you to remember and difficult for others to guess.

Create a Password

(1) Choose Control Panel from the Start menu, click the User Accounts category, and click your account to display the User Accounts window.

(2) In the User Accounts window, click Create A Password.

(3) Type your password, and then type it again to confirm that you didn't make a typing error.

(4) Type a hint that will remind you, but no one else, of your password.

(5) Click Create Password.

> **CAUTION:** Passwords are *case-sensitive*—that is, *MyPASSWORD* and *mypassword* are two different passwords. Make sure that you remember and use the correct capitalization. If you have a problem logging on with your password, make sure the Caps Lock key isn't turned on.

> **TIP:** Windows will ask you whether you want to make your files private only if your computer uses NTFS and you haven't already made the files private.

(6) If Windows asks you whether you want to make your files private, click Yes, Make Private if you want to prevent access by anyone other than yourself to all the files in the My Documents folder and its subfolders.

> **SEE ALSO:** For information about changing a password, see "Changing Your Password" on the facing page and "Resetting Your Password" on page 200.

Changing Your Password

One of the best ways to prevent others from using your account is to change your password occasionally—especially if you gave it to someone or you suspect that someone might have guessed it or watched you type it. When you do change your password, create one that can't be easily guessed (don't use "password" or your well-known nickname, for example), and try to incorporate uppercase and lowercase letters, as well as one or two numbers. Of course, don't make the password so complicated that you can't remember it!

Change Your Password

(1) Choose Control Panel from the Start menu, click the User Accounts category, and click your account to display the User Accounts window.

(2) Click Change My Password.

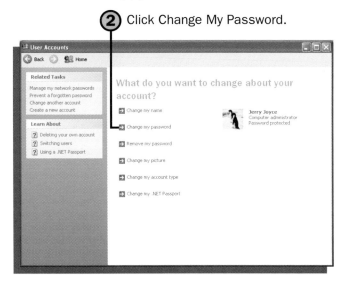

(3) Type your current password.

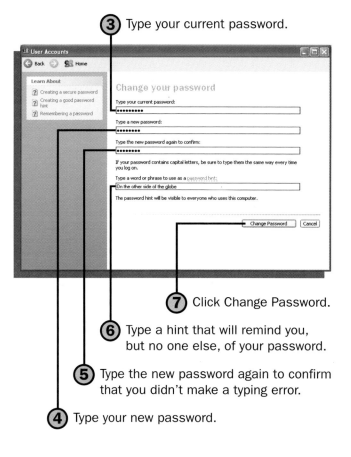

(7) Click Change Password.

(6) Type a hint that will remind you, but no one else, of your password.

(5) Type the new password again to confirm that you didn't make a typing error.

(4) Type your new password.

Resetting Your Password ⊛ NEW FEATURE

Few things are more maddening than trying repeatedly to log on, only to realize that you've forgotten your password! If this happens, you have two choices: you can reset the password (or, if you're a member of the Limited group, you can ask an Administrator to reset it for you), which means that you'll lose all your settings and any security credentials and certificates; or you can use your Password Reset disk to log on and reset your password *and* save all your settings and credentials. The latter is obviously the better choice, so you should create a Password Reset disk while you still remember your password.

Create a Password Reset Disk

(1) Choose Control Panel from the Start menu, click the User Accounts category, and click your account.

(2) Click Prevent A Forgotten Password in the Related Tasks list in the User Accounts window to start the Forgotten Password Wizard.

(3) Step through the wizard, inserting a blank floppy disk in the drive and entering your current password when prompted. When you've completed the wizard, remove the disk, label it as your Password Reset disk, and store it in a secure location.

Reset Your Password

(1) Click here to see your password hint. Enter the password if the hint did its job.

(2) If you still don't remember the password, click here, and, in the pop-up box that appears, click Use Your Password Reset Disk.

(3) Step through the Password Reset Wizard, inserting your Password Reset disk into the drive. When prompted, type a new password and a new (and better!) password hint.

(4) After completing the wizard, type your new password, and press Enter.

Protecting Your Files with a Password

If your files contain sensitive information that you want to protect from prying eyes, place the files in a compressed folder, and create a password. Then, regardless of where those files are located—on your computer, in a shared folder on a network, or on a floppy disk that you lost somewhere—they can be opened and viewed only by you or by someone who knows that password.

TIP: The encryption—that is, the scrambling of text to make it unreadable—of your files can't be cracked unless you're a very sophisticated cryptologist, so make sure you don't forget the password.

Encrypt a Compressed Folder

1 Create and open a new compressed folder. Copy your sensitive files into the folder.

2 Choose Add A Password from the File menu to display the Add Password dialog box.

6 Close the compressed folder.

3 Enter a password. (The password is case-sensitive, so remember your combination of uppercase and lowercase letters.)

5 Click OK.

4 Reenter the password.

7 When you want to access the files, double-click the compressed folder to open it, double-click a file, and enter the password when prompted.

SEE ALSO: For information about working with compressed folders, see "Compressing Files" on page 132.

Restricting User Rights

One of the surest ways to protect your computer from either malicious or accidental damage is to be extremely cautious when you're deciding on the select few who are responsible enough to be allowed full access to the computer. If you're the least bit uncertain, you can always assign people to the Limited group or ask them to log on as Guest users.

Change the Type of Access

1 Choose Control Panel from the Start menu, click the User Accounts category, and click the account you want to change to display the User Accounts window.

2 In the User Accounts window, click the Change The Account Type task.

3 Click the Limited option.

4 Click Change Account Type.

5 Close the User Accounts window.

Use the Guest Account

1 If the Guest account isn't listed on the Welcome screen when you first log on (or when you choose Switch Users from the Start menu), click the User Accounts category in the Control Panel, and click the Guest account.

2 Click Turn On The Guest Account.

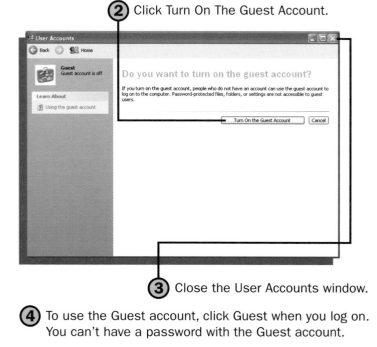

3 Close the User Accounts window.

4 To use the Guest account, click Guest when you log on. You can't have a password with the Guest account.

Protecting Personal Information on the Internet ⊕ NEW FEATURE

Some Web sites that you visit ask you to provide information, such as your name and e-mail address. Others are less direct; they use *cookies*—little text files that are written by the Web site and stored on your computer—to track your activities. Despite their friendly name, cookies can be insidious invasions of your privacy, often using the material they gather for advertising, demographic data, and so on. You can set up Internet Explorer to limit the amount of information you reveal when you're on the Internet.

Set Your Profile

① Start Internet Explorer if it isn't already running, choose Internet Options from the Tools menu, and then click the Content tab of the Internet Options dialog box.

② Click My Profile.

③ Use the different tabs to enter only the information you're willing to reveal to the Web sites you visit.

④ Click OK.

Control Those Cookies

① Click the Privacy tab of the Internet Options dialog box.

② Drag the slider to specify the level of privacy you want. Read the description of the restrictions for that level.

③ Click OK.

④ Try connecting to some of your favorite Web sites. If you're unable to connect, or if the Web pages don't open fully, you might need to adjust your privacy setting. Many Web sites permit access only when you allow cookies; others might not work properly when cookies are disabled.

Restricting Internet Access

The Internet provides access to many things—some weird, some wonderful, and some that might not be appropriate for everyone who uses your computer. To restrict access to certain types of sites—those that contain sexually explicit or violent material, for example—you can use Content Advisor.

Set the Restrictions

1 Start Internet Explorer if it isn't already running, choose Internet Options from the Tools menu, and click the Content tab of the Internet Options dialog box.

2 Click Enable.

8 Click OK.

> ✋ **CAUTION: You must use a password; otherwise, anyone can disable Content Advisor.**

3 In Content Advisor, click a category.

4 Move the slider to adjust the acceptable level of material that can be accessed. Repeat to set levels for the other categories.

5 On the General tab, select or clear check boxes to specify whether unrated sites may be accessed and whether a password may be used to allow access to restricted sites.

6 Click Create Password, enter and confirm your password, provide a hint for the password, and click OK.

7 Click OK.

Configuring an Internet Firewall ⊙ NEW FEATURE

A firewall is a program that's designed to prevent unauthorized and malicious access to your computer over the Internet. In other words, a firewall is your defense against hackers, viruses, Trojan horses, worms, and other slimy evils that slither through cyberspace. Unfortunately, a firewall can also block legitimate traffic, so you might need to tweak the settings a bit. In most cases, the firewall is activated when you create your Internet connection. You can, however, configure the firewall yourself and can turn it on or off.

Configure the Firewall

1 Choose Control Panel from the Start menu, click the Network And Internet Connections category, and click Network Connections in the Control Panel Icon list to display the Network Connections window.

2 Select your Internet connection, and click Change Setting Of This Connection in the Network Tasks list to display the connection's Internet Properties dialog box.

5 Select the check box for each service on your network that needs to bypass the restrictions of the firewall.

3 On the Advanced tab, select this check box to turn on the firewall.

4 Click Settings.

6 Supply the information for each service, and click OK.

7 Click the Security Logging tab, and note the location of the security log.

8 Click OK to close the Advanced Settings dialog box, and then click OK to close the connection's Internet Properties dialog box.

9 Use your Internet connection to make sure it has full functionality. Locate the security log, and double-click it to view any activity that has been blocked by the firewall. If necessary, make changes to your firewall configuration.

Locking Your Computer

If you leave your computer unattended for a while, you can lock it so that even though the programs that were running will continue to run, no one can access the computer using your name. Exactly what happens depends on whether or not you have Fast User Switching enabled.

Lock the Computer

TIP: Fast User Switching is the tool that allows another user to log on to your computer without your having to log off. To enable or disable Fast User Switching, open the Control Panel, click the User Accounts category, and click the Change The Way Users Log On Or Off task.

(1) On your keyboard, press the Windows key + L.

(2) If Fast User Switching is enabled, you'll see the same window that appears when you choose to switch users, and you or another user can log on or resume working.

(3) If Fast User Switching is not enabled, the Unlock Computer dialog box appears, and you can log on using your name, or a member of the Administrators group can log on, causing your account to be logged off.

SEE ALSO: For information about securing the computer using a screen saver, see "Using a Screen Saver" on page 194.

14 Managing Windows XP

The beauty of Microsoft Windows XP is the flexibility it gives you to make changes, fix problems, and generally make your computer work better. If your Desktop is a cluttered mess, you can run a wizard that automatically removes Desktop shortcuts you haven't used for the previous 60 days and puts them in a special folder. If you want to squeeze more items onto your Desktop, you can increase its "virtual" size by changing the screen resolution. If the date or time on your computer is inaccurate, it's easy to change it. If your hard disk is NTFS–formatted, you can compress files, folders, or even the entire drive so that you can store more information in the same location. If your disk isn't NTFS–formatted, you can probably convert it to the NTFS format.

Windows XP also provides disk-maintenance tools that help make your computer run better. You can schedule these tools to run periodically—they'll find and re-order bits of files that have become scattered or lost, delete unused files, and so on. Because computers, programs, and peripheral devices are continually changing, we'll show you how to use the Windows Update Web page to update your computer. You'll learn how to avoid common hardware problems and how to remove software programs. If Windows XP won't start properly, you'll find several solutions that will either get it started or help diagnose what's wrong. If you've made changes to your computer and now wish you hadn't, the System Restore tool will restore your previous settings. And we'll show you how to document your system so that if you do encounter serious problems, you can provide a technician with detailed information about your system.

Adding and Deleting User Accounts

If you're a member of the Administrators group—that is, one who has full access to the computer—you can grant other people access to the computer. You grant access by creating a new user account and specifying whether the account grants full or limited access. To keep things tidy, you can also delete accounts that are no longer used.

Add an Account

1 Choose Control Panel from the Start menu, click the User Accounts category, and click the Create A New Account task to display the User Accounts window.

2 Type a name for the account, and click Next.

TIP: If you save a deleted account's files to the Desktop but don't see the folder containing the files on the Desktop, right-click the Desktop, point to Arrange Icons By on the shortcut menu, and choose Show Desktop Icons from the submenu.

SEE ALSO: For information about the access each type of account allows, see "Know Your Rights, Know Your Format" on page 197.

For information about using the Guest account and about changing the type of account for an existing user, see "Restricting User Rights" on page 202.

3 Click the Computer Administrator option to grant complete access to the computer; click the Limited option to grant limited access.

4 Click Create Account.

TIP: If you want to give someone limited access to the computer for a single session, you don't need to create a new account. Instead, allow the person to log on as a Guest.

Delete an Account

(1) If the User Accounts window isn't already open, choose Control Panel from the Start menu, and click the User Accounts category. In the User Accounts window, select the account you want to delete.

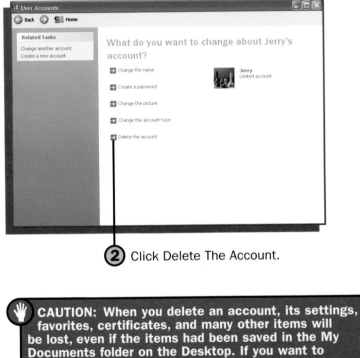

(2) Click Delete The Account.

> ✋ **CAUTION:** When you delete an account, its settings, favorites, certificates, and many other items will be lost, even if the items had been saved in the My Documents folder on the Desktop. If you want to preserve those files and settings, use the Files And Settings Transfer Wizard.

> 👁 **SEE ALSO:** For information about using the Files And Settings Transfer Wizard, see "Transferring Files and Settings" on page 164.

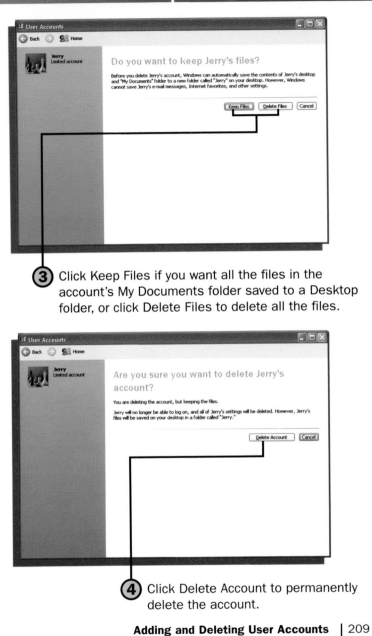

(3) Click Keep Files if you want all the files in the account's My Documents folder saved to a Desktop folder, or click Delete Files to delete all the files.

(4) Click Delete Account to permanently delete the account.

Tidying Up the Desktop ⊛ NEW FEATURE

Although the Desktop is a great place to store shortcuts to files, folders, programs, and Web pages, it can become hopelessly cluttered with items that were probably vital at some point but whose importance is now a vague memory. Do you remember why you placed all those items on the Desktop? Windows XP will take the problem off your hands by removing all the shortcuts that you haven't used for the past 60 days and storing them in a single Unused Desktop Shortcuts folder on your Desktop. You can have Windows run this handy service every 60 days, or you can run the Desktop Cleanup Wizard any time you want.

Start the Cleanup

 Right-click a blank spot on the Desktop, and choose Properties from the shortcut menu.

② On the Desktop tab, click Customize Desktop to display the Desktop Items dialog box.

③ Select this check box, if it isn't already selected, to have Windows XP run the wizard every 60 days.

④ Click the Clean Desktop Now button, and click Next to start the Desktop Cleanup Wizard.

⑤ Clear the check boxes for any shortcuts that you *don't* want removed from the Desktop and placed in the Unused Desktop Shortcuts folder, and click Next.

⑥ Review the shortcuts that will be deleted, and click Finish.

Changing the Date or Time ⊕ NEW FEATURE

Windows XP and your computer keep track of the date and time, using commonly accepted formats to display them. If the date or time on your computer is inaccurate, or if you travel with your computer into different time zones, you can quickly adjust and correct the settings.

Change the Date or Time

(1) Double-click the time on the taskbar to display the Date And Time Properties dialog box.

(2) If necessary, on the Time Zone tab, select a different time zone, and make sure the Automatically Adjust Clock For Daylight Saving Changes check box is selected or cleared, depending on whether or not the region you're in uses Daylight Saving Time.

(3) Click the Date & Time tab, and click the correct month or year in the list if necessary.

(4) Click the correct date if necessary.

> **NEW FEATURE: Windows XP can link to a time server on the Internet so that the time on your computer is always accurate. If your computer is always connected to the Internet, its time will be adjusted automatically once a week. (If you connect to the Internet manually, you can update the time yourself.)**

(5) Click the Internet Time tab. If you aren't already connected to the Internet, connect now.

(8) Click Update Now, and wait for the time to be updated.

(9) Click OK.

(7) In the list, click the time server you want to use.

(6) Select this check box if it isn't already selected.

> **! TIP: If the time isn't displayed in the notification area of the taskbar, right-click a blank spot on the taskbar, choose Properties from the shortcut menu, and select the Show The Clock check box.**

Changing the Display

If you want to squeeze more items onto your Desktop, you can change its size…sort of. This is one of those "virtual" realities. You "enlarge" the available space by changing the screen resolution, and thereby the *scaling,* which lets you fit more items onto the Desktop even though its area on your screen doesn't get any larger. Your gain in virtual area comes at a cost, though—everything will be smaller and harder to read. Also, the combination of screen resolution and color quality displayed affects how much video memory (the memory on your computer that's dedicated to producing the video image on your monitor) is used. Therefore, you might need to adjust both the screen resolution and the color quality until you're happy with the result.

Increase the Screen Area

1 Right-click a blank spot on the Desktop, and choose Properties from the shortcut menu to display the Display Properties dialog box.

2 On the Settings tab, drag the slider to specify a screen area (the degree of screen resolution).

Preview the change in the Desktop area.

3 Specify the color quality you want to use.

4 Click OK.

5 If the Monitor Settings dialog box appears after you've changed the Desktop, click Yes to accept the new settings or No to revert to the original settings. If you don't click Yes within 15 seconds, Windows restores the original settings.

TRY THIS: Click the Advanced button on the Settings tab, and, on the Adapter tab, click the List All Modes button. Review the many modes in the list, and select one that has the resolution, color quality, and refresh rate you want. A different refresh rate might reduce or eliminate any flicker on your screen. Click OK, and confirm that you want to use the current settings.

TIP: If text is too large or too small after you adjust the screen area, click the Advanced button on the Settings tab, and change the font size.

Compressing a Drive or a Folder

When a disk is formatted for NTFS (NT file system), you can compress its files and folders—and even the entire drive—so that you can store even more information in the same location. The cost of compression can be a slightly longer time to access files, which must be decompressed before you can use them. This delay is usually so minor, however, that you won't even notice it on most systems.

Compress a Drive

1 Open the My Computer window, right-click the drive you want to compress, and choose Properties from the shortcut menu to display the drive's Properties dialog box.

2 On the General tab, select this check box to compress the drive.

3 Click OK.

4 Click the first option if you want to compress only the root directory of the drive (that is, no folders will be compressed); click the second option if you want to compress all the folders and files on the drive.

5 Click OK.

Compress a File or Folder

1 Right-click the file or folder, and choose Properties from the shortcut menu. On the General tab of the Properties dialog box, click the Advanced button to display the Advanced Attributes dialog box.

2 Select this check box to compress the file or folder.

3 Click OK, and then click OK again to close the Properties dialog box.

4 Click the first option if you want to compress the folder only; click the second option if you want to compress all the subfolders and files in the folder.

5 Click OK. Wait for the files and folders to be compressed.

Changing the Disk Format

Windows XP supports three disk formats—FAT, FAT32, and NTFS. The NTFS format provides the speed, resources, security, and ability to handle large disks that aren't available with the FAT or FAT32 formats. The FAT and FAT32 formats provide compatibility with other operating systems (dual-boot or multi-boot configuration, or the backup of a previous operating system) running on your computer. If your hard disk uses FAT or FAT32, and if you're certain that compatibility won't be an issue, you can convert the disk to the NTFS format.

Convert the Disk

1 Back up your work, and then close all the files and folders on the disk you're going to convert.

2 Click the Start button, point to Programs and then Accessories, and choose Command Prompt from the submenu to display the Command Prompt window.

> **SEE ALSO: For information about checking the format of the drives on your computer, see "Know Your Rights, Know Your Format" on page 197.**

7 Close the Command Prompt window.

4 If you upgraded your computer from a previous version of Windows, type **Y** and press Enter to confirm that you want the backup deleted, or type **N** and press Enter to terminate the procedure.

5 If you're notified that the system can't gain access to the drive and are asked whether you want to force a dismount of the drive, type **N** and press Enter.

3 At the command prompt, type **Convert drive: /FS:NTFS /v** (where *drive* is the drive letter of the hard disk or drive to be converted), and press Enter.

6 If you're told that the system can't gain exclusive control (as is the case when the drive is the primary drive), type **Y** and press Enter to convert the drive when the system restarts.

8 Choose Turn Off Computer from the Start menu, click Restart in the Turn Off Computer dialog box, and wait for the computer to restart and convert the drive.

Maintaining Your Computer

With time and use, your computer can become a bit disorganized. As the information stored in your computer gets used, moved, copied, added to, or deleted, the computer's drives can become cluttered with useless or inefficiently organized files. Windows XP provides a group of maintenance tools whose occasional use can make your computer run more smoothly, more efficiently, and (usually) faster. The table at the right describes what each of these tools does.

Maintain the Drives

① Choose My Computer from the Start menu, right-click the drive that needs attention, and choose Properties from the shortcut menu to display the drive's Properties dialog box.

Local Disk (C:) Properties

General | Tools | Hardware | Sharing

Error-checking
This option will check the volume for errors.
Check Now...

Defragmentation
This option will defragment files on the volume.
Defragment Now...

OK | Cancel | Apply

Disk-Maintenance Tools

Tool	What it does
Disk Cleanup	Checks the disk for unused files that can be deleted.
Error-Checking	Scans the disk to see whether there are disk errors in any files or folders. Optionally, fixes file-system errors and attempts to recover bad sectors on the hard disk. If the disk is in use, error-checking will be scheduled for the next time you log on. For NTFS–formatted disks, records all file-transaction information.
Defragmentation	Analyzes the disk to see whether defragmentation is necessary. Re-orders the items on your disk so that files aren't separated into several noncontiguous parts. Can take a long time to run but speeds up disk performance.

② Click the appropriate button to use the tool you need, and follow the instructions provided by the program:

- On the General tab, click Disk Cleanup.

- On the Tools tab, under Error-Checking, click Check Now.

- On the Tools tab, under Defragmentation, click Defragment Now.

SEE ALSO: For information about managing unused shortcuts on your Desktop, see "Tidying Up the Desktop" on page 210.

Controlling the Power Options

Different computers sometimes have different power-management requirements and abilities. You might want the monitor on your main desktop computer to shut down after a few minutes of idleness, but you might also want the hard disk to "stay awake" constantly.

On your portable computer, you might want everything to shut down after a few minutes of idleness. Depending on the features and abilities of your computer, you can set these power schemes, as well as some other features.

Use a Power Scheme

(1) Choose Control Panel from the Start menu, click the Performance And Maintenance category, and click the Power Options Control Panel icon to display the Power Options Properties dialog box.

(2) Click a power scheme in the list.

(3) If the preset power schemes don't meet your specific needs, modify the settings. Click Save As, and save your settings as a new scheme.

Set Advanced Options

(1) Click the Advanced tab of the Power Options Properties dialog box.

(2) Select this check box if you use a password to log on and you want the security of requiring the password to be entered whenever the computer is revived from Standby or Hibernate mode.

(3) Specify the actions you want to occur when you press the various power buttons.

(!) TIP: Power settings are primarily controlled by the ACPI (Advanced Configuration And Power Interface) features of your computer. Windows XP has very strict standards for supporting ACPI. If, even though your computer is designed to support ACPI, Windows doesn't enable the ACPI features, contact the computer manufacturer for updates that might make your computer's ACPI system work with Windows XP.

Set Battery Options

① Click the Alarms tab, and set the battery level at which the computer will take action. Click Alarm Action for each alarm to specify what happens when the battery reaches the specified level.

③ Select this check box if you want to see the details about each battery.

② Click the Power Meter tab, and check the current power level of the battery or batteries.

Set Other Options

① Select the appropriate check box on each of the following tabs:

- APM to enable the APM feature when the ACPI feature isn't available on the computer
- Hibernate to enable hibernation
- UPS to configure the settings for any Uninterruptible Power Supply attached to the computer

② Click OK when you've finished.

> **!** TIP: You'll see the Alarms tab and the Power Meter tab only if your computer is a portable computer with a battery. You won't see the UPS tab on a portable computer. The APM tab appears only on computers that have the APM (Advanced Power Management) feature and don't support the ACPI feature.

Updating Your System

As time marches on, Microsoft continues to make improvements, fix problems, and offer new features in Windows. Windows XP keeps track of which updates you need for your computer. You can choose to have Windows automatically check for new updates over the Internet, or you can check for updates by visiting the Windows Update Web page. Either way, the updates are downloaded to your computer, and then you can install them.

Specify How You Want to Update

1 Click the Stay Current With Automatic Updates message when it appears, and click Next to start the Automatic Updates Setup Wizard.

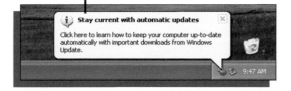

TIP: To set up or change the way you receive updates at any time, choose Control Panel from the Start menu, click the Performance And Maintenance category, and click the System icon. Change your settings on the Automatic Updates tab of the System Properties dialog box, or choose to install updates that you previously chose not to install.

CAUTION: When you install updates, make sure that you're the only person logged on to your computer, and that you have closed all your running programs. Although this isn't necessary in all cases, some updates require you to restart the computer, which could cause other people who are logged on to lose some of their work.

TIP: Automatic updates work best when your computer is continuously connected to the Internet or when you remain connected for long periods of time. If you dial in for short Internet sessions, it's easier to use manual updates.

 2 Click an option to specify whether

- You want updates to be downloaded automatically.
- You want to be notified so that you can select the updates you want.
- You want to turn off automatic updating.

3 Click Next, and then click Finish to complete the wizard.

4 If you chose to download updates automatically or to be notified about available downloads, follow the instructions on the screen to download and install the updates.

Update Manually

1 Choose Windows Update from the All Programs submenu of the Start menu. Connect to the Internet if you aren't already connected.

2 Have Windows Update scan your computer for any items that need to be installed. If prompted, install any software tools from Microsoft that are needed to complete the scanning and cataloging of your computer.

 CAUTION: Don't believe any stories you might hear that Windows Update spies on your computer. The only information you send to Windows Update is your choice of which items to install. All the other information (the catalog of your installed items) is stored on your computer and is never sent to Windows Update.

3 Review the items to be installed. Select the check boxes for the ones you want to install, and clear the check boxes for the items you don't want to install.

4 Click Install Now.

If you want to review either the items you've already installed or other updates, select this task.

5 Wait for the update or updates to be copied to your computer and installed. Follow the instructions on the screen, and, if instructed, click Yes to restart the computer.

Preventing Hardware Problems

Diagnosing hardware problems can be a time-consuming and expensive activity. Instead of checking and modifying settings, uninstalling and reinstalling drivers, and replacing hardware devices that might or might not be incompatible with Windows XP and/or with your computer system, you can avoid most problems by being cautious about any hardware you install, and by using it properly.

Prevent a Problem

(1) When buying hardware, make sure that it's certified to work with Windows XP. Many older items and some discounted items aren't designed to be used with Windows XP. To search through a list of devices that have been tested for full compatibility with Windows XP, choose Windows Catalog from the All Programs submenu of the Start Menu.

(2) Install only hardware drivers for hardware devices that are designed for Windows XP and that are digitally signed (indicating that they're authentic). When you're manually installing a hardware device, you'll be notified if the driver isn't digitally signed.

Safely remove USB CompactFlash II - Drive(E:)
Safely remove TOSHIBA CD-ROM XM-7002B - Drive(D:)
2:28 PM

(3) When you're using certain devices, such as some USB (Universal Serial Bus) and SCSI (Small Computer System Interface) devices, you must stop the device before it can safely be removed. To stop a device, click the Safely Remove Hardware icon in the notification area of the taskbar, and then click the device to be stopped and removed.

SEE ALSO: For information about identifying hardware problems, see "Documenting Your System" on page 224 and "Managing Everything" on page 225.

TIP: If a device driver isn't digitally signed, check with the manufacturer for an updated driver. Many drivers that were designed for use with Windows 2000 might work correctly with Windows XP. However, you can't be certain that a device is fully compatible unless it's certified for Windows XP and is digitally signed.

CAUTION: One of the most frequent causes of a sudden hardware problem is something called "surprise removal." This happens when you remove or disable a hardware component when it's in use or when your system thinks it should be available. If you want to undock a portable computer from its docking station, for example, you should either use the Undock Computer command on the Start menu, or shut down the computer and turn it off before you undock it. If you're using a USB hub, don't disconnect its power supply, don't turn off the hub's power, and don't remove any components from the hub while Windows XP is still running.

Removing a Software Program

Most programs are *registered* with Windows XP when you install them. You can—and should—use Windows tools to remove a program. If you simply delete the files, you might leave accessory files you don't need, or delete files you need for other programs. When you uninstall a program using Windows tools, Windows keeps track of the files, and only when a file is no longer needed by any of your programs does Windows delete the file.

Uninstall a Program

① Close all your running programs. Choose Control Panel from the Start menu, and click the Add Or Remove Programs category to display the Add Or Remove Programs dialog box.

② Click Change Or Remove Programs.

③ Select the program you want to remove.

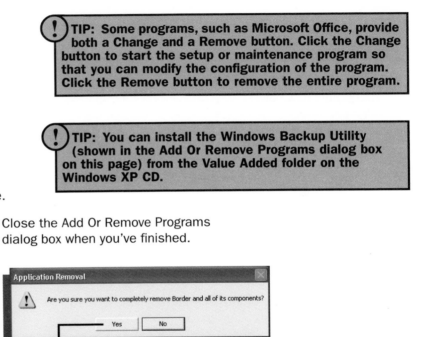

④ Click Change/Remove.

> **SEE ALSO:** For information about removing programs that came with Windows, see "Adding or Removing Windows Components" on page 166.

> **TIP:** Some programs, such as Microsoft Office, provide both a Change and a Remove button. Click the Change button to start the setup or maintenance program so that you can modify the configuration of the program. Click the Remove button to remove the entire program.

> **TIP:** You can install the Windows Backup Utility (shown in the Add Or Remove Programs dialog box on this page) from the Value Added folder on the Windows XP CD.

⑦ Close the Add Or Remove Programs dialog box when you've finished.

⑤ Confirm that you want to remove the selected program. If another program starts and offers you a choice of actions, use it to remove the selected program.

⑥ Wait for the program to be removed, and then click OK.

Starting Up When There's a Problem

If you have a problem starting up Windows XP correctly, you can use one of several startup procedures either to determine what's wrong or to start Windows with minimal features so that you can adjust or restore settings. After you've started Windows, you can use a variety of techniques to fix whatever is wrong with the system.

Control the Startup

1 Restart your computer.

2 After the computer system loads, and as Windows XP starts, hold down the F8 key. (If your computer displays a list of operating systems, press F8 when that list appears.) The Windows Advanced Options Menu appears.

3 Use the Up arrow key to select Safe Mode.

4 Press Enter.

5 Make changes to your system to correct the problem.

6 Shut down your computer, and then restart it to see whether it starts correctly now.

7 If the computer doesn't start correctly, repeat steps 1 and 2, and choose a different startup mode to help diagnose the problem.

 SEE ALSO: For information about fixing problems by resetting your computer to the previous settings, see "Fixing System Problems" on page 223.

CAUTION: If Windows XP came preinstalled on your computer, read the computer manufacturer's documentation about fixing problems before you execute any actions.

TIP: If you believe the computer isn't working properly because of changes you just made to the system, choose Last Known Good Configuration from the Windows Advanced Options menu to restore the system's previous settings.

Startup Options

Option	What it does
Safe Mode	Starts with no network connections and without most of its drivers.
Safe Mode With Networking	Starts with network connections but without most of its drivers.
Safe Mode With Command Prompt	Starts without network connections, without most of its drivers, and with the command prompt only.
Enable Boot Logging	Starts normally; records startup information to the *ntbtlog.txt* file (in the Windows folder).
Enable VGA Mode	Starts normally but uses only the basic VGA video driver.
Last Known Good Configuration	Starts normally using the settings stored in the Registry when the computer was last shut down properly.
Directory Services Restore Mode	(Not available for Windows XP Home Edition.)
Debugging Mode	Starts normally but sends the debugging information to another computer over a serial cable.
Start Windows Normally	Starts Windows as if you hadn't pressed the F8 key.
Reboot	Restarts the computer.
Return To OS Choices Menu	Goes to the menu to select operating system to start.

Fixing System Problems

A fabulous feature of Windows XP is the System Restore tool, which makes it possible for you to undo whatever changes you or programs have made to your system. Periodically, and whenever you make changes to the system, Windows records all the system information. If you've made changes to the system but the effect isn't what you wanted, you can tell Windows to revert to the previous settings.

Restore the System

 Close all your running programs, and make sure that no one else is logged on to the computer.

② Choose System Restore from the System Tools submenu of the Start menu to display the System Restore window.

④ Click Next.

③ Click the Restore My Computer To An Earlier Time option.

⑤ Select a date that contains a restore point. (Only the dates in bold type contain restore points.)

⑥ Click the restore point you want to use, and click Next.

⑦ Review the item that's being restored, and then click Next to start the restoration process. Wait for the settings and any files to be restored, and log back on when prompted. Click OK when you're notified that the restoration has been completed.

Documenting Your System

Be prepared! Even if your system is working perfectly now, the day might come when you'll encounter a problem that you can't fix yourself. When you need professional assistance, you're going to have to supply a helpful technician with as much information about your system as possible. Windows XP can provide you with a vast amount of information about the system, and you can document some or all of it. Much of the information is indecipherable to the average computer user, but it's invaluable for the support person. Some of the system documentation can be useful to you, though—you might need to refer to it when you're planning to add items to or remove them from the system.

! TIP: The Tools menu contains some powerful and advanced tools for monitoring and modifying your system, and you should know how these tools work before you attempt to use them. To learn about them, either search for information in Windows Help And Support, or start the tool and use its Help program.

Get the Information

1 Choose System Information from the System Tools submenu of the Start menu to display the System Information dialog box.

2 To record all the information about your system, click System Summary. To limit the information to a specific component, click that component in the list.

3 Choose Export from the File menu, and save the information as a text file.

4 Use the text file as your external source of information about your system. You can e-mail the file to a technician, save it on another computer or on a floppy disk, or use Notepad or WordPad to edit, format, and print relevant portions of the report.

Managing Everything

Windows XP provides a powerful administrative tool called the Computer Management Console that gives you access to almost everything on your computer system. You can use this tool to explore your computer and learn about the adjustments you can make, and—armed with a little knowledge—you can then use the tool to maintain and improve your system.

Use the Console

1 Right-click My Computer on the Start menu, and choose Manage from the shortcut menu to display the Computer Management Console.

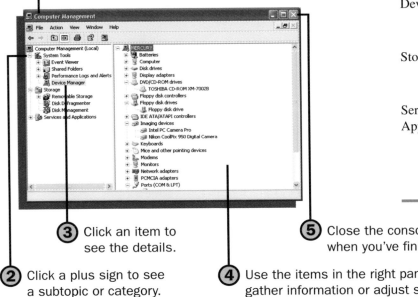

3 Click an item to see the details.

2 Click a plus sign to see a subtopic or category.

5 Close the console when you've finished.

4 Use the items in the right pane to gather information or adjust settings.

Computer Management Console Items

Item	What it does
Event Viewer	Allows you to view logs of events (including errors and warnings) for your applications, security, and the operating system.
Shared Folders	Monitors which items on your computer are shared on the network, who's currently connected to your computer, and which files are being used.
Performance Logs And Alerts	Provides technical data about the running of the computer.
Device Manager	Lists all hardware devices on the system. You can adjust settings, including installing or uninstalling new device drivers.
Storage	Provides information about removable and fixed disks, and allows some management of those disks.
Services And Applications	Lists all the services available on your computer; allows you to manually start or stop services; and provides access to the Indexing Service, where you can manage the service and directly query the index of files on your computer.

Helping Each Other ⊕ NEW FEATURE

How many times have you screamed "Help!" (or worse) when your computer was being an uncooperative brat, only to be met by silence? Now your pleas for help won't disappear into the void. Using the Remote Assistance feature, you can contact someone over the Internet for help. Your friend or coworker can view your computer Desktop, can review your system information, and can even chat with you to help you figure out what's wrong. Likewise, if a friend or colleague has a problem that you know how to solve, you can be the expert who provides the oh-so-welcome assistance.

> **TIP:** To ask for help from someone who isn't in your Contacts list, choose Other from the Ask For Remote Assistance submenu, and type the person's e-mail address.

Ask for Help

1 Start Windows Messenger if it isn't already running, log on, and open the Windows Messenger window. Point to Ask For Remote Assistance on the Tools menu, and choose the contact from whom you want help. Wait for that person to accept the invitation, and then confirm that you want him or her to view your screen and chat with you.

2 When you're connected, type a message to explain your problem, and press Enter.

3 If you want to discuss the problem using audio, click Start Talking.

4 If the person asks to take control of your computer, click Yes to allow him or her full access to the computer and permission to make changes to the system. Click No if you want to retain control and make changes or act on suggestions yourself.

5 If you've allowed the other person to take control of the computer, click Stop Control (ESC) when you want to terminate that control.

6 When you've finished (and solved the problem, we hope!), click Disconnect to end the remote assistance.

Give Help

① With Windows Messenger running, log on, and wait for the invitation to provide help. When you receive it, accept the invitation, and wait for the Remote Assistance window to appear.

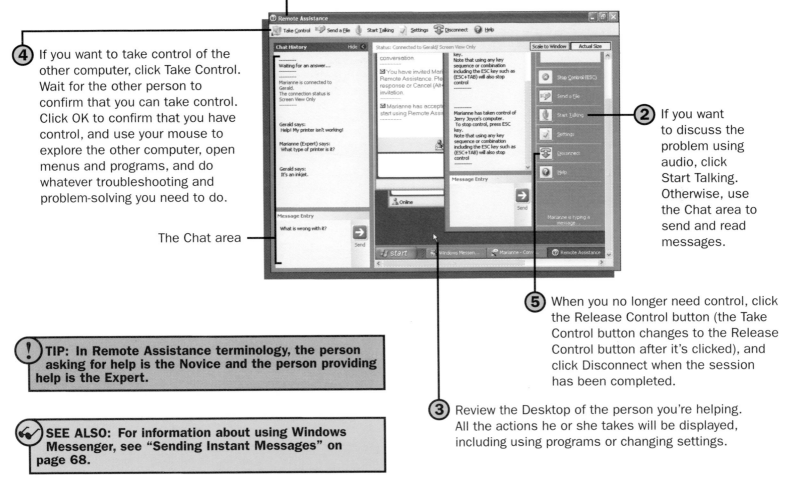

④ If you want to take control of the other computer, click Take Control. Wait for the other person to confirm that you can take control. Click OK to confirm that you have control, and use your mouse to explore the other computer, open menus and programs, and do whatever troubleshooting and problem-solving you need to do.

The Chat area

② If you want to discuss the problem using audio, click Start Talking. Otherwise, use the Chat area to send and read messages.

⑤ When you no longer need control, click the Release Control button (the Take Control button changes to the Release Control button after it's clicked), and click Disconnect when the session has been completed.

③ Review the Desktop of the person you're helping. All the actions he or she takes will be displayed, including using programs or changing settings.

> **! TIP:** In Remote Assistance terminology, the person asking for help is the Novice and the person providing help is the Expert.

> **SEE ALSO:** For information about using Windows Messenger, see "Sending Instant Messages" on page 68.

Editing Windows XP Settings

Windows XP uses a database called the *Registry* to keep track of all its settings, including most of the programs that are installed on the system. Occasionally—if there's a problem with your system or with a program, or if you simply want to customize the system—you'll need to modify the contents of the Registry.

CAUTION: Because any modifications to the Registry can cause systemwide problems, you should modify the contents of the Registry only if you have detailed instructions from a reliable source, and—as everyone will warn you—at your own risk and only after you've backed up the Registry.

Edit the Registry

1 Choose Run from the Start menu to open the Run dialog box.

2 Type **regedt32** in the Open box, and click OK.

3 Choose Find from the Edit menu to display the Find dialog box.

4 Type the name of the *key* you're looking for.

6 Click Find Next.

5 Select the Keys check box if it isn't already selected. Clear the check boxes for Values and Data if they're already selected.

7 Check the directory structure to verify that you have the correct key. If it's not the correct key, choose Find Next from the Edit menu until you've located the correct key.

8 Double-click the item you want to change.

10 Close the Registry Editor, and see whether the change works as expected.

9 Make your changes, and click OK.

TIP: A key is an identifier for a record or a group of records in the database. The Registry edit shown on this page disables the AutoComplete feature at the command prompt when you press the Tab key.

Index

Send feedback about this index to
mspindex@microsoft.com.

A

access control. *See also* passwords
  encrypted files and folders, 203
  private files and folders, 196, 198
  user groups, 197, 202
accessibility tools, 192–93
account pictures, 191
accounts
  e-mail, 170–71
  user (*see* user accounts)
ACPI, 216
Active Desktop. *See* Desktop
Add A Contact Wizard, 67
Add Favorite dialog box, 46, 48
Add Hardware Wizard, 176
Add Network Place Wizard, 147
Add Printer Wizard, 173
Address Bar, Internet Explorer, 44
Address Book, 11
  adding addresses from messages, 64
  creating contacts, 64
  creating groups, 65
  importing addresses from other
    address books, 65
  online contacts, 67
Address toolbar, 144
administrative tools, 225
Administrators group, 197, 208
Advanced Configuration And
  Power Interface, 216

alarms, battery level, 217
album information, downloading, 98
Align To Grid option, folder views, 129
alternative input options, 192–93
Alt+Tab key combination, 14
annotating faxes, 123
APM option, 217
appearance
  of folders, 129–31, 189
  of Windows Media Player, 99
  of Windows XP, 178–79
applications. *See* programs
arithmetic operations, 29
attachments, receiving and sending, 58, 59
audio. *See also* CDs
  accessibility tools, 192–93
  associating sounds with events, 110
  audio clips, 108–9
  audio conversations, 69
  audio tracks, adding to movies, 92–93, 94
  controlling volume, 104
  music CDs, 98, 100, 101
  Narrator, 106
  playing audio files, 102, 103
  reading documents using Narrator, 106
  sound files, creating, 107
Audio And Tuning Wizard, 69
Audio CD dialog box, 98
Auto Arrange option, folder views, 129
auto-hiding taskbar, 186
automatic actions
  arranging windows on Desktop, 16
  updating Windows XP, 218
automatic fax reception, 120
Automatic Updates Setup Wizard, 218
AutoPlay behavior, 190

B

Back button, 13, 44
Backgammon, 38
background colors and pictures, 180
backing up data, 138–39, 140–41
Backup program, 166
battery options, 217
bitmaps
  BMP format, 76
  editing individual pixels, 78
  file size, 77
BMP format, 76
booting Windows XP, 8, 222
bridges between networks, 150
Briefcase, 66
browsers
  Internet Explorer, 44–51
  MSN Explorer, 52
burning CDs, 140–41
business cards, electronic, 65
buttons
  customizing appearance, 179
  taskbar buttons, 186
  on toolbars, displaying, 144

C

Calculator, 11, 29
Called Subscriber Identifiers (CSIDs), 172
canceling print jobs, 115
card games. *See* games
case sensitivity of passwords, 198
cd command, 30

229

Q

R

S

About the Authors

Jerry Joyce has had a long-standing relationship with Microsoft: he was the technical editor on numerous books published by Microsoft Press, and he has written manuals, help files, and specifications for various Microsoft products. As a programmer, he has tried to make using a computer as simple as using any household appliance, but he has yet to succeed. Jerry's alter ego is that of a marine biologist; he has conducted research from the Arctic to the Antarctic and has published extensively on marine-mammal and fisheries issues. As an antidote to staring at his computer screen, he enjoys traveling, birding, boating, and wandering about beaches, wetlands, and mountains.

Marianne Moon has worked in the publishing world for many years as proofreader, editor, and writer—sometimes all three simultaneously. She has been editing and proof-reading Microsoft Press books since 1984 and has written and edited documentation for Microsoft products such as Microsoft Works, Flight Simulator, Space Simulator, Golf, Publisher, the Microsoft Mouse, and Greetings Workshop. In another life, she was chief cook and bottlewasher for her own catering service and wrote cooking columns for several newspapers. When she's not chained to her computer, she likes gardening, cooking, traveling, writing poetry, and knitting sweaters for tiny dogs.

Marianne and **Jerry** own and operate **Moon Joyce Resources**, a small consulting company. They are coauthors of *Microsoft Word 97 At a Glance, Microsoft Windows 95 At a Glance, Microsoft Windows NT Workstation 4.0 At a Glance, Microsoft Windows 98 At a Glance, Microsoft Word 2000 At a Glance, Microsoft Windows 2000 Professional At a Glance, Microsoft Windows Millennium Edition At a Glance, Troubleshooting Microsoft Windows 2000 Professional,* and *Microsoft Word Version 2002 Plain & Simple.* They've had a 20-year working relationship and they have been married for 10 years. If you have questions or comments about any of their books, you can reach them at moonjoyceresourc@hotmail.com.

The manuscript for this book was prepared and submitted to Microsoft Press in electronic form. Text files were prepared using Microsoft Word 2002. Pages were composed using Adobe PageMaker 6.52 for Windows, with text set in Times and display type in ITC Franklin Gothic. Composed pages were delivered to the printer as electronic prepress files.

Cover Graphic Designer

Tim Girvin Design

Interior Graphic Designers

Joel Panchot, James D. Kramer

Interior Graphic Artist

Kristin Ziesemer

Typographer

Kristin Ziesemer

Proofreader/Copy Editor

Alice Copp Smith

Indexer

Caroline Parks (Indexcellence, Inc.)

Get a **Free**

e-mail newsletter, updates,
special offers, links to related books,
and more when you

register on line!

Register your Microsoft Press® title on our Web site and you'll get a FREE subscription to our e-mail newsletter, *Microsoft Press Book Connections.* You'll find out about newly released and upcoming books and learning tools, online events, software downloads, special offers and coupons for Microsoft Press customers, and information about major Microsoft® product releases. You can also read useful additional information about all the titles we publish, such as detailed book descriptions, tables of contents and indexes, sample chapters, links to related books and book series, author biographies, and reviews by other customers.

Registration is easy. Just visit this Web page and fill in your information:

http://www.microsoft.com/mspress/register

Microsoft

- -

Proof of Purchase

Use this page as proof of purchase if participating in a promotion or rebate offer on this title. Proof of purchase must be used in conjunction with other proof(s) of payment such as your dated sales receipt—see offer details.

Microsoft® Windows® XP Plain & Simple

0-7356-1525-X

CUSTOMER NAME

Microsoft Press, PO Box 97017, Redmond, WA 98073-9830